"In a series of poignant, well-crafted essays, Cindy Eastman writes about her life before, during and after taking care of her elderly father. Her experiences show caregivers that they are not alone with their fluctuating feelings of guilt, anger, sadness and joy. But this is way more than just a book for caregivers. It is a story of love between a daughter and her father. One that everyone can benefit from reading."

—JANIE EMAUS, Author of the picture books, *Latkes for Santa Claus* and *Easter Eggs and Matzo Balls* and the adult novel, *The Advice Columnist.*

"Both cautionary tale and how-to manual, Cindy Eastman's collection of essays on caring for her elderly father in her home is a 'real-time' chronicle of the madness (and the occasional joy) that accompanies the honorable and deeply challenging endeavor of caring for a loved one. We are treated to honest storytelling that will resonate with all family caregivers in the murky middle of the journey. Every family caregiver will recognize themselves in this humorous, vulnerable, questioning memoir of life on the frontline. And feel less alone."

—GRETCHEN STAEBLER, author of *Mother Lode: Confessions of a Reluctant Caregiver*

"A courageous memoir about the dark side of caregiving. Eastman took on the care of her elderly father by having him 'move in with her family' but discovers over time that in reality, 'her family moved in with him.' As a psychotherapist who works with caregivers in the areas of cancer, neurological diseases, and dementia, this memoir is a reassuring read to anyone who has struggled with the complexities of caring for another human being. Eastman writes of the frustrations, the guilt, the exhaustion, and the difficulties of maintaining one's own life as a caregiver, and brings attention to the serious issues of aging and eldercare in the United States. It is only recently that the significant concerns surrounding caregiving and the crucial needs of caregivers has been recognized. A reassuring read for those who are in the role of caregiver."

—CHERYL KRAUTER, MFT, author of *Surviving the Storm, Psychosocial Care of Cancer Survivors, Odyssey of Ashes*

TRUE
CONFESSIONS
OF AN
AMBIVALENT
CAREGIVER

TRUE CONFESSIONS OF AN AMBIVALENT CAREGIVER

A MEMOIR IN ESSAYS

CINDY EASTMAN

SHE WRITES PRESS

Published 2024
Printed in the United States of America
Print ISBN: 978-1-64742-718-4
E-ISBN: 978-1-64742-718-4
Library of Congress Control Number: 2024910026

For information, address:
She Writes Press
1569 Solano Ave #546
Berkeley, CA 94707

Interior Design by Tabitha Lahr

She Writes Press is a division of SparkPoint Studio, LLC.

Company and/or product names that are trade names, logos, trademarks, and/or registered trademarks of third parties are the property of their respective owners and are used in this book for purposes of identification and information only under the Fair Use Doctrine.

Names and identifying characteristics have been changed to protect the privacy of certain individuals.

To my family, the ones who are still here
and the ones who have gone on.
Especially Annie.

CONTENTS

After

PREFACE

The goal of my book is twofold: first, to share my particular perspective with others who might feel the same, and second, to start a national conversation on services and resources available to aging elders and their families.

Caring for an elder relative, especially a parent, is rife with conflicts. Everyone has heard the old saw that gets pulled out at these times: "Well, they took care of you, now it's time to take care of them" or some variation of that theme. This, to me, is a false equivalence that brings with it too many situations that can cause even more conflict.

No two births are alike, no two deaths are alike, and neither are the journeys we make from cradle to grave. I believe that we as a society and culture can improve how we look at and care for our elders. There are just too many places where our attention is lacking, and this most important segment of our society—the keepers of history—goes unattended, some more blatantly than others.

As I write this, the national conversation under President Biden appears to be shifting its focus to include caregiving for our vulnerable populations: children and elders. I hope it means that we'll see more services, oversight, and research into how to best care for our aging population. They deserve it. We *all* deserve it.

INTRODUCTION

"It was the best of times, it was the worst of times, it was the age of wisdom, it was the age of foolishness, it was the epoch of belief, it was the epoch of incredulity, it was the season of Light, it was the season of Darkness, it was the spring of hope, it was the winter of despair, we had everything before us, we had nothing before us, we were all going direct to Heaven, we were all going direct the other way . . ."

—CHARLES DICKENS, famous caregiver

The essays in this collection will hopefully tell the story of the main conflict that arose when I decided to have my 86-year-old dad move in with my husband Angelo and me after my mom died. I am writing it while in the thick of it because when I am not a caregiver anymore, meaning when Dad dies, I might not be able to retrieve the memories and experiences I am going through right now. Or I might not be as open and honest about recording them through the lens of loss and grief. Right now, almost every day can be a struggle, and it occurred to me that it might seem harsh to write about these problems as it could appear disloyal or even cruel on my part to share such intimate details of our lives together. Giving up the family secrets while the family is still around to find out about it might offend or hurt someone, particularly my dad. But I'm not going to tell him.

Of course, it isn't my intention to be disloyal, but it might seem like that to some. I want to share the difficulties I face to possibly give even one other person in the same situation some affirmation. It's not all altruistic, however. As a writer, writing is how I process my experiences to give them meaning. Writing about my experience will help me get through it, one way or another. Not every caregiver's situation is the same because no two people are alike. Throw in some aging, grief, ancient family dynamics, and a few medical issues, and every day is walking through another landmine field without a helmet. Right now, it sounds like it's all bad, and it's not. There are some good days, and there are some bad days.

I am writing this story even though I know it will reveal some of the really bad decisions I make and some of the unpleasant characteristics I have. For all the caregivers out there who can handle being growled at or who give up their privacy, I applaud them. I really do. When I find myself once again snapping back at Dad because he snapped at me because I had to correct something he did wrong, I could kick myself. I wonder how someone else would handle this, even as I know what is driving his sarcasm or defensiveness. He is forgetful and vain, generous and angry. These are not really compatible attributes, and it makes caring for someone difficult. But not just any someone—a daughter and her father.

It might seem like deciding to have my dad come and live with my family and me was the first bad decision. I don't think so. But there were plenty made after that. I'll even tell you about most of them. But that first decision, the one that set off the most difficult and challenging time of my life, is one I'd probably make again and again. Therein lies the conflict: I thought I was having my dad come live with us when actually we now live with him in our home.

BEFORE

MY DAD

*Published in the Newtown, Connecticut
Newtown Bee June 1995*

" I love you." The phrase elbowed itself in between "Don't forget to send in that insurance form" and "Will talk to you soon." My dad.

My mother called last week. She sounded almost conspiratorial when she said, "Your father is in the living room watching the news, so I decided to call so *I* could talk to you! If he knew I was on the phone with you, he'd come in here!"

The funny thing about all this is that for nearly all my thirty-six years, my mother was the one who did all the talking. On the phone, in letters, over coffee late on the first night home from college. My dad communicated through prompt tuition payments, an extra five-dollar bill in a rare note, oil changes for our cars, and clipping our fingernails before church on Sundays. Stoic was the word I always thought of for him, with an incredibly dry and well-developed sense of humor.

As a child growing up, I was always aware of him as a presence in our home but not so much as a person. On Saturdays, my younger brother, sister, and I would clamor to be the one to get to go into work with him. Years later, my mother told us, "I always told him he could work on Saturday, but he had to be home before noon!" I guess he figured that since it was such a brief time, one of us might as well accompany him. We would get up early, go for a doughnut, and arrive at the sprawling, intimidating Appliance Park in Louisville, Kentucky. A huge place—to us the size of Cleveland—where many of General Electric's refrigerators, stoves, and other assorted appliances were assembled and tested. This place didn't seem to intimidate him, though.

We drove past building after building the size of airplane hangars until he knew just where to pull in. He knew the right door and had the right key. I would follow in awe down darkened hallways to his office. He would get right to work and leave us to our own amusements. Office supplies in abundance were our rewards for assisting him at work, and we had access to a treasure trove of markers, pens, and paper with which to draw, color, and write. I think a stop at the Burger Queen on the way home tied up the adventure like a nicely wrapped present.

As we got older, the trips to GE lost their appeal, but his communication continued in driving lessons, constant safety reminders that still play over and over in my head ("The car is not a toy. If you're thirsty, drink water."), and his droll funny stories and jokes at Thanksgiving and Christmas dinners. My mother acted as the interpreter and speaker of the house. "You know how your dad feels about that!" and we'd nod solemnly but not really have a clue. We knew where he grew up (Cromwell, Connecticut), where he went to school (Wesleyan University), where he worked (GE), what he was (a chemist), and the music he loved (classical), but I don't think any of us knew how he felt.

I knew how he sang though. One of my fondest memories is standing next to him in church, listening to him sing with a deep baritone voice that his deaf sister-in-law could hear over the phone. His voice came right from his soul, and his devotion and dedication to the church remained unchallenged. Church was important to him, and we knew that.

Then it was off to college. I went 2,000 miles away to Austin, Texas. He'd loaned me his college trunk, which I felt proud to have until I got off the plane and saw the faces of the students who were assigned to help the incoming freshmen (*This is yours?!*). I have kept it with me ever since. It's bulky and huge, but it's my dad's. At school, I received letter after letter from my mother. Care packages, notes, poems, love. Every six months or so, my dad would write a note. In it, without fail, was an article from the *New York Times* or *Newsweek* about how to get along in college on five dollars a week or how Austin, Texas, was just rated the best place to live or study habits for a straight-A term. "Just a few brief lines," he'd write and send his love through the articles.

I got married and became pregnant with my daughter. She was due on January 8th, so that's when my scientist-minded dad came to visit me. He had to leave a few days later—but Annie did not cooperate with his travel plans, and he didn't meet her. So, my dad came back to Austin on a business trip in April. Annie was just four months old but had already been hospitalized with viral meningitis a month before. My dad scooped her up in his arms and spent most of his time with her for the entire trip. As I watched them together, I felt that maybe that's what he had been like with me as a baby.

During another trip, this time to visit my parents in Connecticut, he scolded me one evening for being too hard on Annie and attributed her "bad" behavior as a normal response to my driving her crazy! Finally, a comment about my parenting after all those years, and it was a negative one! But it came from a source that had never been open to me as a child and was only tapped as grandchildren began appearing.

After my daughter Annie, came my son, Christopher, and then my sister's son, John. Saturday morning errands with the grandchildren replaced the go-to-GE trips with Dad. With list in hand as he walked out the door with Annie (or Christopher or John) was the inevitable question: "Anyone need anything?" Coming back into the house from such a trip, one or two of the bags were items from the list and at least one additional bag was packed with multicolored cereals, snack packs of pudding, soda, coloring books, ice cream, stuff "the kids might like" (including himself, of course). A few years later, my dad was diagnosed as a diabetic, and he was *supposed* to cut down on that kind of thing, but he's never let his diabetes put too much of a dent in our need for treats. He wasn't going to let anything get in the way of his expressions of love.

He forged a trail through the woods to the woodpile behind their house with Christopher, he introduced Annie to his love of New York City, and John benefited from living in Middletown and enjoyed "Papa's" connection to that town. Special trips to New Haven, breakfasts at the coffee shop on the green, and the Essex Christmas train were the things he did with his grandkids. My dad even braved the Connecticut Post Mall at Christmas to take the boys to see the Teenage Mutant Ninja Turtles! At Christmas time! This is a mall with hundreds and hundreds of screaming kids belonging to pushy parents with video cameras. I can safely say I would *never* have done that.

Years ago, during my divorce, I saw another side of my dad. My parents had loved Bob and taken him into our family. Now I was asking them to end that relationship as I ended mine. One night, during the beginning, painful, accusatory stage, Bob called me from Interstate 95 outside of New Haven and said he was going to do something to spare us from all this pain. Would I please look out for the kids and tell them he loved them, but he just couldn't go on anymore.

I was insane with worry. I called the state police and then I called my dad. He lived in Guilford, an hour and a half away, and immediately got in the car and came to be with me. We waited. At two o'clock in the morning, I was awakened and looked out the window. Bob had returned. He was just standing by his car in the chilly November morning, smoking a cigarette. I woke my dad, who had also dozed off, and he got right up and walked outside. I watched as he walked right up to Bob, hugged him, and led him inside. Unbelievable! I was hoping he would punch him out! But he hugged him!

Looking back from this vantage point, I see that is how he always was: fair and loving. I had never experienced it quite like that from anyone else I had ever known. My mother was openly loving: hugs, kisses, tears, and giggles. My dad not so much. But there he was, all the time. Responsible, reliable, strong, smart. Now, with all the wisdom my thirty-six years brought me, I see how he was with people was a good thing. Hugging Bob was a fair and loving thing to do. The burden of being his child was that he always expected that of us. To look beyond the surface of others to their pain beneath. As children, we thought he didn't care. As grown-ups who have inherited that sensitivity, tempered with my mother's openness, it's obvious that to love like he does requires much strength. The gift of being his child is that we were raised to be just like him. It's harder to be like that within our own family because we all possess inherited intuitiveness, and we tend to be somewhat like a family of empathetic porcupines. Our mother taught us to love everyone, and my dad taught us to always do the right thing. It's a formidable task. We, my dad's children, have no choice. We are just like him.

I wouldn't want to be any other way.

COUNTING BLESSINGS

*"The secret of happiness is to count your blessings
while others are adding up their troubles."*
—WILLIAM PENN

One cold January day—my dad's birthday, in fact—I was alerted by the town manager of the island where my family has a cottage that a spate of break-ins and vandalism had occurred. Since the island is on a lake in Maine, it becomes inaccessible for about six months of the year, when the lake freezes over, to the owners and renters who are fortunate enough to take advantage of its lush green golf course and deep blue waters from about April to November. The alert was in an email sent out to owners (and owners' daughters) that the police had been called and we would hear further about whether our cottage had been "hit." The local handyman, who keeps an eye on things during the winter, let us know that he would check on our place, but there was little else to do, as the burgled cottages were crime scenes. If necessary, he would secure the cottage against further incursion from the elements and animals that are the island's typical winter residents.

Frye Island is a small one-by-three-mile island on which my parents bought a "fixer-upper" cottage for their retirement. It was during a family vacation when we saw a sign that said, "lake view lots on Frye Island." We were intrigued—an island? We had to go see it. We drove around and around on this little island looking at cottages. Some on the water, some in the middle of a bunch of pines. Then we drove up a driveway to this funny-looking place. Like two shoeboxes fallen askew next to each other. My mom sat in the car with a look on her face that declared, "I don't think so." Then the real estate agent said, "This one needs someone with real imagination."

Mom bolted out of the car and walked in the front breeze-way. From there, you could see straight out to the lake at the foot of a decrepit stairway and out to Mount Washington beyond. At the time, the view was the best thing about the place. One didn't need a real imagination; one needed a complete departure from reality to be able to visualize what to make of this place. Enter my mom, the female St. Jude. She started looking a little more intently at the possibilities. Meanwhile my dad and I picked our way among the rocks at the shore with three-year-old Annie. We met back at the agent's car, and Dad said wistfully, "I've always wanted a place on a lake that overlooked Mount Washington."

St. Jude just looked at him with one of those looks, as only a saint of hopeless causes can give.

Since then, our family has a cottage on a lake that we can only visit six months of the year, and largely ignore for the other six months. Until this year. Once I got the emailed notice and checked in with the handyman, I figured I'd get in touch with Mom and Dad to see if they had heard about the crimes. I finally reached them. It was Dad's birthday so they had been out most of the day—crazy partiers. Yes, they had gotten the email, and as Mom, Dad, and I chatted about it on speakerphone we all expressed the same thought: desperate times call for desperate measures.

We decided it was hard to be angry about a situation like this. I was sitting in my (nearly) warm home, mortgage paid and food in the pantry; my parents were safe in their lovely retirement community in sunny Florida; and someone up in Maine thought that finding a way across a frozen lake to break into empty cottages was a good way to make some money. All of the homes on the island are second homes. No one lives there year-round. No one can. There's no electricity or internet access. No heat, no boats, no grills barbecuing hot dogs and hamburgers. Someone was in such dire straits that risking a plunge into the icy water or abandonment on a deserted, frozen island didn't seem as bad as a house with no heat or a table without food. It could have been kids. Kids are dumb like that sometimes. If it's kids, we'll probably see a video montage of their feat on YouTube. If it's a guy trying to pay the bills, probably not.

The emails from the town manager continued throughout the week, and the last one indicated that if we hadn't been contacted directly, our cottage was probably okay. During the conversation with my parents, my mom cracked that the vandals had probably taken one look at our place and said, "Nah . . . there can't be anything worth something in that one." And on a purely economical level, they'd be right. Take the TV, the DVD player, or the printer, but there's nothing else of value in the place. Most of everything in the cottage was there when my parents bought it decades ago. And that stuff had been there for a decade before that.

We're not talking about a Newport cottage here; it was an old fishing camp that someone slapped a few doors on. In fact, the burglars could have backed a truck up to the house and carted away almost everything there and not have made a dent in what was really important. And that's exactly what Mom, Dad and I talked about that night on his birthday. What could they take? Nothing that couldn't be replaced. The most important thing we had was the place itself and the love and the memories therein. If someone needed our TV, our electronics, or the printer, then they should take it. Good luck; get a good price. If there is one thing that our family knows for sure, it's that we know a blessing when we have one.

THE LONG AND WINDING ROAD

*"Whoever wants to reach a
distant goal must take small steps."*
—Saul Bellow

(Or drive a small golf cart . . .)

I don't remember why, but I was the only one visiting my parents one Fourth of July weekend in Maine, and we were going to do what everyone does on Frye Island that weekend: head to Long Beach and watch the fireworks show. We had been enjoying a streak of picture-perfect Maine summer sunniness—so it was on.

A day earlier, my dad drove our golf cart up to the front of the house, liberating it from underneath the giant blue tarp it usually sat under, and announced, "We'll take it up to the fireworks." We acquired the golf cart years ago after we sold the Boston Whaler that came with the cottage. We tried to be boaters, we really did, but boating just wasn't in us. So, off went the Whaler, and in came the cart. Now that was a vehicle that got some use. You could buzz down to the store for a paper, run up to the community center for a ceramics class, or get rid of a couple of bags of garbage without disturbing the dust on anyone's car.

When my son Christopher spent two summers on the island scooping ice cream cones at the little store, the golf cart was his preferred and constant mode of transportation even if it wasn't exactly street-legal. However, once he got a real driver's license, the golf cart was as neglected as the Velveteen Rabbit. But, we hauled it out every spring to clean and gas it up, ready for service, only to be dusted off and returned to its place under the tarp in the fall with very little use in between.

So, it was a bit of a surprise to see Dad drive it up to the front of the house, not because we didn't often use it, but because he actually didn't drive anymore. And probably shouldn't have been. Over the years, due to diabetes, my dad's eyesight grew more and more compromised. He had to give up driving—even the golf cart—and we all knew it made him feel useless, although he didn't talk about it that much.

But there he was, futzing around with the lights, cleaning pine needles off the seat, testing the battery. He was getting the cart ready for the fireworks show like a teenager anticipating his first date.

After the cleaning, he came into the kitchen and said to no one in particular, "I'm just going to take it down the road and back—see how it's working," and he was off. Mom and I just looked at each other, like, "What could possibly happen?" I wondered how many hazards there could be in the rutted, rock-strewn dirt road up to the corner and back, so after he safely made it out of the driveway, I sat on the front porch, waiting for him. The better to hear any loud crashes or shrieks of terror that way.

About six hours later, he returned. Or maybe it was six minutes. Either way, I let out the breath I didn't realize I'd been holding. "All set!" he said, and he walked back into the living room to read, as if taking the cart for a spin was something he did every afternoon.

We didn't talk about it at dinner, so I figured the test run was the extent of his driving for the day and I'd be chauffeuring us all to the fireworks. It wasn't until I heard him shout from outside, "Everyone ready to go?" that I realized he intended to drive us as he was planted firmly in the driver's seat.

At the last minute, Mom stayed back. "Something at dinner didn't agree with me," she said with her hand on her belly. Nerves about my dad being behind the wheel? Possibly. It could also be that she didn't want to sit on my lap all the way to Long Beach. In any case, she begged off, promising to call if she felt better.

I took my place on the passenger side. My dad turned the key, kicked off the brake, and hit the gas. We were off. Down the driveway—great. Up to the corner—well, he had already practiced that one, hadn't he? Right onto Leisure Lane and the open road. Should I keep my eyes open or squeeze them shut? Leisure Lane winds about a mile from our road to the town beach. A dirt mile of sharp turns, gallon-sized potholes, scattered rocks of varying sizes bordered by boulders, low-hanging pine branches, and occasionally, toddlers.

At first, I tried being a helpful navigator. "Family of six up on the right," I said.

"See it," Dad said.

"Enormous truck bearing down on us on the left," I yelped.

"Got it," he said.

As we took each turn and steered past cars parked alongside the road, I realized—we were doing okay. Compromised eyesight or not, the one thing my Dad had always been was responsible. I knew he wouldn't do anything he didn't think he could do, especially if it meant it might put me—or anyone—in harm's way. Deciding to get behind the wheel was a decision he probably thought through very carefully, so I relaxed my grip on the seat handle and let him drive.

We parked as close to the beach as possible, just another cart among the dozens that had made their way there that night. We unpacked our folding chairs and found a spot in the sand right by the water. We settled in, chatted with neighbors, and waited for the show to start. Staring up at the dazzling display, I couldn't tell what Dad was thinking, but I bet he felt relieved. On the return trip, I drove and Dad navigated. In the dark, with all the dust kicked up by departing firework-watchers, seeing was difficult enough for my fifty-plus-year-old eyes, much less for seventy-five-year-old eyes dimmed by diabetes.

I walked down to the dock while Mom, suddenly cured, fixed coffee and dessert. I stuck my feet in the water and was delighted to notice a couple of fireflies dancing and twinkling below the branches of a white pine about ten feet in front of me. Sometimes, the little things are really the most impressive.

IN AN INSTANT

"Life changes fast. Life changes in the instant.
You sit down to dinner and life as you know it ends."
—Joan Didion

I was in Florida again, only weeks after my previous trip in February. Not because I'm a member of the elite class that can fly at a whim to wherever in the world is the most comfortable weather-wise, but because my dad was in the hospital. They were fine when I left Mom and Dad that Thursday afternoon a short two weeks earlier. They were planning on heading down to the dining room with the rest of the Bay Village residents for the burning of the deed—the mortgage was paid off and everyone was getting cookies and champagne to celebrate. A happy note on which to leave.

This trip was not so happy to make. The very day after I left, Dad fell, hit his head, and began a journey for which there was no map—for all of us. At the hospital, side effects from the concussion gave him aspiration pneumonia, which triggered a coma. My sister Susie had been in Florida on the opposite coast, and while getting ready to fly home, called Mom and got the news. She canceled her plans and drove across the state to be with our parents. My brother Richard and I relied on her reports of Dad's progress until we made our own arrangements to fly to Florida, coincidentally arriving within minutes of each other; me from Connecticut, and he from California. I rented a car, and we drove straight from Tampa to Sarasota Memorial Hospital where we found our exhausted mom and sister and unresponsive dad.

After that first life-changing call, our lives continued to change over the next few weeks. In the first few days, we had all the difficult conversations: locating the advance directives, honoring my dad's wishes, and planning for the future. It was draining. And then that final, awful conversation—to take out the ventilator. After it was removed, we all squeezed around my dad's bedside and held our collective breaths as the doctor quietly asked him if he could raise his arm. Suddenly and robustly, he flung his arm up in the air as high as he could, up and down, three or four times. Yes, he could!

I don't remember exactly what we did, but I think we all cried. And then came the other conversations: choosing rehab, affording home care, who was staying, who was leaving, etc. The five of us had been together in recent years but within our larger, extended family. Operating as the original five in an emergency was the family dynamic on steroids. Our common focus was, of course, Dad. Secondary to that was Mom and her health. And we were doing all of it on top of each other. We three siblings kept getting in each other's way, outdoing the next in being helpful and considerate. I offered some imagery to help us keep some perspective: we were all floating in the pool of our love for our parents but on separate rafts, with separate needs and feelings. Clearly, we would probably bump into each other on occasion, but it would just be a slight bump from a serenely floating raft, and we could float off in another direction without turning it into a big deal. It seemed to work.

On we went, figuring out where to stay (What? It's spring break? Who knew? About a million northerners, that's who). My parents lived in a one-bedroom apartment with a fold-out sleeper in the living room, so one of us could stay there. Susie won the long straw on that one. Bay Village offered guest rooms, but the spring break thing affected their availability, too. Plus, their rates, like every single hotel in town, were crazy-expensive. Richard and I were nomads, hauling our belongings with us as we inquired at every hotel within walking distance of the hospital. A family friend offered their home and car to me for a few days, and it was like a life preserver (to continue with my pool analogy) as it gave me the solitude I needed to process our experience. Friends of my parents loaned us their car, pretty much indefinitely, while we were all there: a gold Sebring convertible. They were worried we wouldn't like it, but we drove everywhere with the top down like we were teenagers. Our cousins offered a bed and meals, and all in all, we were pretty well taken care of. Which was a good thing, because none of us really knew what we were doing except for just wanting to be there.

As Dad began regaining his consciousness, but not his memories, we hung around him day in and day out, just to catch the next thing he was going to say. We laughed more than we cried. One day I was Olga, his sister. As far as anyone knows, there was never a sister or an Olga. I was back to Cindy the next day. One morning he shared with Susie that he was surprised that the nurses brought him his breakfast in French maid costumes. We gently suggested to him that it could have been a "waking dream" as French maid's outfits aren't exactly conducive to proper medical care. Mom kept running her hand over the stubble that was growing on Dad's face and remarking how handsome he was—as if she had forgotten. Richard took some of the overnights and learned that Dad's stubbornness was intact: he pulled out his feeding tube more than once.

Eighteen days after the fall, Dad was back at Bay Village in the rehab wing conveniently located one floor below my parents' apartment. On the night before I left—begrudgingly, to go home—the staff arranged it so we could all have dinner together in a private room. Dad asked us all to hold hands as he expressed his gratitude that we were all able to be there together. He said he was grateful that we all loved each other and that we all liked each other, too. "And not necessarily in that order," he added, smiling.

For the first few days I had been away from home, I had occasional tugs of responsibility. But those tugs were quickly brushed away as I turned my attention to flagging down a nurse or finding lunch for Mom. I was lucky that my husband Angelo, my kids, and my friends took up the slack when I left for Florida with only a one-way ticket and no idea what was going to come about. The emergency consumed me. I am not someone who jumps on a plane and leaves home for an unknown length of time, but that's just what I had done. When lives change in an instant, it is often due to a calamitous or devastating event that forces us to rally our energy and resources to make sense of our lives once more.

What if we could do that same thing, but mindfully, with purpose? Could I change my life in an instant? Once I returned home, the only thing I thought about was my next trip to Florida. Not that I had been invited, but I planned on going anyway. After an emergency like that, it was clear my parents would need some additional assistance, whether they wanted it or not. Mom was never a big fan of my so-called help, but I think even she thought it might come in handy. In a weak moment, she admitted to me, "I kind of miss having you all around to get some errands done." Changing my life intentionally to include caring for my parents wasn't something I ever considered, but now? I think that's what life-changing is all about.

DECISIONS

". . . we're all mad here."
—CHESHIRE CAT TO ALICE
famous bad decision-maker

The first realization hit me early on in our new arrangement—
it became clear that there was a big difference in what we
had decided to do as compared to what we were actually
doing. When Angelo and I discussed the decision with the
family, we talked about "having Dad come to live with us."
After Mom died, my brother and I took turns staying with
Dad in the one-bedroom apartment in the luxury retirement
facility my parents had moved to about five years earlier—
and, to be fair, my brother bore the lion's share of care; I only
subbed in a couple of times. When we stayed with Dad, our
own lives were suspended while we hung out in the twelve-
story pink high-rise my parents had called home. There were
two dining rooms, a pool (that the residents rarely used), an
exercise room, a shady walk around a pond, and an enviable
location in Sarasota, Florida.

When I was there, I shelved the responsibilities and chores
that occurred in my daily life; of course I did—there was a lot

to be done, and I was hundreds of miles away from my home in Connecticut. I still figured I'd grab a couple of hours here and there to work. As a writer—and as many people like to remind me—I can write anywhere! How lucky was I that I could do it in beautiful Sarasota! But I could barely attend to my emails. I clearly remember thinking that, if I were at home, this would be so much easier because I could attend to my work, my family, and my life and still take care of my dad. This tempting thought figured largely into our decision-making to have Dad move north with us. As we discovered quickly, it was inaccurate.

What really happened was this: Dad didn't come live with us, blending in with our schedules, our commitments, and our social engagements. We now live with him—in our home. The way Angelo and I lived our lives before my dad moved in now must work around an entirely different schedule and a new level of needs.

It's a subtle but significant distinction. Discovering this hasn't made me regret my decision; in fact, it helps now that I have a clearer understanding about what we've gotten ourselves into. For a while, I thought I could continue working on my book, run my writing retreats, pick up a couple of classes, and still work part-time with my husband in our parenting program. The half dozen or so other commitments I had inked into my calendar—meetings mostly, from the casual coffee with a friend to the numerous town committees on which I serve—would have to be turned back into pencil. Or sometimes, canceled.

We were empty nesters for many years before my dad moved in. As a result, Angelo and I both created a flexible schedule with abundant time to share. Our home was big enough to modify, and we had a desire to help. It seemed like an ideal situation. We felt very grown up and pragmatic about making this decision. We knew we couldn't anticipate everything, but we felt whatever did come up, we could handle it. That seemed reasonable.

What I learned, however, was sure, we can handle things that come up, but effectively handling the events that pop up on a consistent basis while also trying to maintain a demeanor of calm and competence is draining. Even anticipated situations required a greater level of energy and patience than I've ever had to draw on, even more so than when I was a single parent twenty-five years ago. Decisions we made that seemed like a good idea at the time ended up being pretty bad decisions. For example, sending my husband off to Italy for three weeks seemed like a good way to stay committed to our plan of visiting his hometown for at least a month each year; a plan we had only commenced the year before. (He ended up staying since we knew we couldn't turn a bad decision into a good one by simply reversing it.) So, we're learning as we go. The biggest thing I learned is that even though the whole family was involved in the decision to bring my dad into our home, the caretaking responsibility largely rests on one person. In our case, it's me.

PATRICIA ERLE EASTMAN

Farley Funeral Homes and Crematory
OBITUARY OF PATRICIA ERLE EASTMAN

Patricia Erle Russell Eastman of Sarasota, Florida, died peacefully on January 15, 2017, at Tidewell Hospice of Sarasota after a brief illness. Known as Pattie, she was born on December 21, 1933, in New Rochelle, New York. She attended Mary Burnham School in North Hampton, Massachusetts, and Katherine Gibbs Academy in New York City. After graduation, Pattie worked for Rayonier in the Chrysler Building in NYC.

In 1956, she married Warren Eastman, and together they had three children: Cindy, Richard, and Susan. After marriage, Pattie devoted her time and energy to raising their three children. Her professional skills were used in her volunteer work, beginning at Springdale Presbyterian Church in Louisville, Kentucky, where she and Warren also led the church Youth Group. She also worked for a time for a local psychologist managing his practice. Once Warren was relocated back to Connecticut, Pattie continued giving her time to the Guilford Free Public Library, The Mercy Center, and many projects at their church. She earned a CNA certificate, volunteered at a nearby nursing home, and spent many years working with SARAH, an agency that provides programs and services for people with intellectual and other disabilities.

When Pattie and Warren retired to Osprey, Florida, Pattie's volunteering continued in her work with their church, St. Andrew's UCC, and the many organizations with which she and Warren became involved. Resurrection House, SURE, Habitat for Humanity, and Hospice benefited from her commitment to helping others, a facet of her nature that was her signature quality. Volunteering wasn't the only outlet; her poetry and drawings will continue bringing inspiration and love to those fortunate enough to have experienced it. A gentle soul, Pattie was creative, funny, and loving, and she will be greatly missed by her family, friends, and community. Pattie is survived by her husband, Warren Eastman, and their children Cindy, Richard, and Susan. She is survived by her grandchildren Annie, Christopher, Justine, and John, and her great-grandchildren Luca, Madeline, and Aiden. Her loss also impacts Angelo, Stephan, Tony, and Adam, and her longtime friend Pris. Funeral arrangements are being handled by Farley Funeral Home. A memorial service will be held at 11 a.m., St. Andrew's UCC of Sarasota on Tuesday, January 24, 2017. In lieu of flowers, memorial donations may be made in Pattie's name to the St. Andrews Church Memorial Garden or Tidewell Hospice Sarasota, Florida.

WOE: DAILY SCHEDULE

This document was left in a folder whenever Dad's care was left to anyone else.

	MEAL/SNACKS	ACTIVITY	NOTES
MORNING	Breakfast Cereal & ½ Banana w/packet of Stevia Diet Juice in fridge Coffee—black (OJ for low blood sugar ONLY) Under 60	Take Novolog (per scale on back of Dexcom)—1 unit Take Tresiba (13 units) Take AM pills— (the NOON compartment is a sublingual Vit. B taken in the AM with breakfast.)	Check for correct dosage on insulin pens Check the correct pill compartment is taken Check for correct side for insulin injection (opposite of Dexcom transmitter)
LUNCH Typically 1–2p.m.	Sandwich Bowl of soup (½ can of Progresso) Activia yogurt Diet cookie Diet soda—pantry	Check blood with Dexcom Take Novolog per scale	Soup in cupboard above tea kettle Yogurt in fridge Soda in pantry-bottom shelf Cookies in bread drawer
AFTERNOON Typically 4 p.m.	MiraLAX Cheese crisps (BS 180^) or Wheat Thins (BS 180v)	MiraLAX	Crystal Light to mix MiraLAX in fridge MiraLAX & cheese crisps in cupboard Wheat Thins on top of fridge
EVENING	"Cocktails"—snacks and wine spritzer (sometimes beer or Scotch & water) Dinner Dessert—Golf-ball-sized ice cream is okay	Check blood sugar via Dexcom Take Novolog per scale—adjust for low reading (under 150 subtract a unit)	Snacks on top of fridge
BEDTIME Typically 10 p.m. (before brushing teeth)	½ bottle of Glucerna (in fridge or pantry)	Take p.m. pills Eye routine 4 Glucose tabs next to bed (just in case)	Pills in paper cup Eye drops and ointment next to bed

Note:

Warren can typically administer his insulin and meds on his own; however, each of these needs to be monitored in case of mistakes. Make sure he puts the correct pills in his cup, winds up the insulin pen to the correct number, takes the correct number of units (the chart is on the back of the Dexcom unit), etc. Do not ever hesitate to ask to look at any of these things if you think he has miscalculated or has the wrong dosage.

Insulin/Dexcom Notes:

Please Note: sometimes it takes up to an hour before the glucose takes effect and impacts the blood sugar reading.

The Dexcom is a Continuous Glucose Monitor that reads data from a transmitter affixed to Warren's left side. All insulin injections should be delivered on the right side.

The extra pens for both insulins are in the fridge on the bottom shelf on the left. Novolog is the fast-acting insulin he takes with meals, and Tresiba is the insulin he takes once each day in the morning.

When in doubt, use the Blood Glucose Meter (in the cigar box). This is the truest reading of his blood sugar. He uses a fingerstick to draw blood, inserts a test strip into the meter, and touches the strip to the blood on his finger. All supplies for this are in the cigar box. He typically knows how to do this, but often needs assistance.

Medications:

His medication tray is on the top of his closet in his room. It will be filled up for the week. He usually takes out the correct sleeve for the day, but I put the pills in a little paper cup next to the cigar box on the counter. It's still a good idea to watch him take his pills.

The supply of meds is in the black canvas case, also on top of the closet.

Meals

Breakfast: Cereal is on the shelf next to the fridge. All Warren's "supplies" are on the top right shelf of the fridge: Almond milk, OJ (for low blood sugar only), diet juice, **MiraLAX**, etc. He usually has cereal with a half a sliced banana, a packet of Stevia, and almond milk. He takes his coffee black. Coffee supplies are in the cabinet to right of the oven. On Saturdays and Sundays, he gets eggs and waffles.

Lunch: Usually a sandwich, soup, and a diet yogurt. Diet Pepsi. He has a sugar-free cookie afterward—in the bread drawer.

Dinner: Warren is used to having a "cocktail" before dinner, usually a half a glass of white (or red) wine mixed with seltzer water. He has "Pattie Puffs" (salted caramel corn puffs on top of fridge) or some pretzels, chips etc.

Dinner can be anytime from 6 to 8 p.m. as balanced as possible. He shouldn't have any dessert if dinner is carb-heavy (pasta, potatoes, rice, bread, etc.). However, if dinner is on the early side, he might have a small scoop of ice cream (the size of a golf ball) or a cookie around 9 to 9:30 p.m.

All backup supplies are in the pantry (kitchen door foyer). There is Glucerna, ICE water, cereal, crackers, etc. Beverages are on the bottom shelf.

iPhone/iPad:

His Dexcom app is connected to his iPhone. Both need to stay charged and within several feet of him throughout the day to register readings. He uses his iPad in his room to listen to his audiobooks on tape. The app is Bard, and he knows how to access it. He might need help finding new books.

Camera:

We have a few cameras in the kitchen. Nothing needs to be done with these, just letting you know that they are there.

Exercise:

Warren has a manila folder with sheets of exercises he needs to do for his physical therapy. He has used the treadmill in the past but doesn't use it alone. He should have some water if he exercises. I have asked Warren to not exercise if no one is in the house. Nor should he shower when he is alone.

Other Supplies:

Depends are in a package next to the nightstand in Warren's room. I keep about four at a time in his top dresser drawer. The baggies he uses for disposal are also in the top drawer of his dresser. There are also backup supplies on the shelf in the bathroom for toothpaste, Fixodent, etc. There are additional supplies on a shelf in the basement to the right of the stairs.

Batteries for the blood glucose meter, hearing aids, headphones, etc., are in the bottom drawer of his closet. There are also extra needles and test strips in that drawer.

MORNINGS

I was already bitchy about losing an hour of sleep to "spring forward" when I saw Dad pop into view on the kitchen "Dad cam," dressed and ready to go at 8:00 a.m. It was my fault, of course. I set his clock forward before he went to bed instead of leaving it at "fall back" time and conning him into staying in bed another hour. Instead, he was up and at 'em and ready to start his day. When his day starts, so does mine.

The countdown begins when I see him go into the bathroom. He'll spend about twenty minutes in there. Once he gets back into his room and I hear him—over the baby monitor—tell Alexa to turn on the light, I have another twenty minutes or so before he takes his place at the kitchen counter to begin his daily routine: fill his pockets, blood test, calibrate, insulin shots, and meds. Then, breakfast, coffee, and check his phone. Every morning.

It never helps if I am already cranky at having to get up earlier than usual. Each morning he needs to test his blood sugar, have his glucose monitor calibrated, take his meds, and inject two different types of insulin. At any point in the routine, something can go awry. This usually leaves him feeling frustrated or "embarrassed," and then he gets defensive or sarcastic. Keeping my crankiness in check is up to me, but that doesn't always guarantee success. Most days, we do okay. Sometimes, I want to run screaming from the house.

There are many ways in which this routine can crash and burn. First, he or we test his blood sugar on the blood glucose monitor. Dad usually manages this pretty well as long as he can grab just one thin, inch-long test strip from the vial, insert the correct end into the meter, get a viable drop of blood out of his finger, aim the small test strip into that drop, and get a reading. Once he gets a reading, we calibrate that number with the one on his Dexcom glucose monitoring device. This is one of my jobs, as unlocking the device, navigating to the right menu item, and inputting the information requires a little more dexterity and speed than he has available to him in the morning. Or ever.

Once calibrated, Dad's attention turns to his shots. There are two of them: a long-lasting insulin, and an as-needed fast-acting insulin. So far, he can do this on his own, too, usually without incident. But since there *have* been incidents, he needs supervision. The long-acting insulin is the same number of units every morning, unless the endocrinologist changed it at the most recent appointment. That's usually good for a couple of weeks of, "It's fourteen units? I thought it was twelve?"

Both insulins come in a pre-filled pen with a little dial at the bottom to set the right amount, which is shown in a little window near the bottom of the pen. The numbers are small, so it only shows the even ones, which works okay on the long-acting, but when it's time for the fast-acting, we can run into trouble. For example, per his dosage scale, if his blood sugar reads between 110 and 150, Dad takes five units of insulin with his meal. Winding up the pen to five is always tricky since he can't really see it. But we like to have him do the things he can still do. For example, he's still able to screw the needles onto the pen, but he has to remember to inject himself on the side of his stomach opposite the CGM (continuous glucose meter) that is attached just above his hip on his side. The CGM sensor is replaced each week, so the injection sites alternate weekly. This will all change once the CGM is upgraded, but for now, it's one more thing we—and by "we" I mean I—have to remember to do.

Next . . . meds.

Of the daily meds nestled in the four-compartment box, the five in the MORN compartment get swallowed together. He then pops the dissolvable Vitamin B from the NOON box under his tongue and walks the Levothyroxine from the EVE compartment into a little black cup in the bathroom so he can take it first thing the next morning when he wakes up to pee. If he remembers. The BED box holds another five pills to take at bedtime with a glass of Glucerna.

Usually, it all goes as planned, but one day he took the p.m. pills instead of the a.m. Another time he added a couple of extra units to the slow-acting insulin, and yet another time—when he ran out of the fast-acting insulin—he needed a new pen for the remaining six units of the dose and nearly injected himself with the full fourteen units instead. Recently he mixed up Vitamin B with the Levothyroxine and slipped the Levothyroxine under his tongue and placed the Vitamin B in the black cup. I caught that one in time and he simply spit it out. None of the mistakes are immediately life threatening— all can be reconciled throughout the day with modifications and attention. However, if I make sure they all get completed properly, it means not adding extra duty throughout the rest of the day.

I understand he gets frustrated when he makes a mistake, but it is also frustrating to hear him respond with negativity and intolerance for a pretty basic human condition—aging, and its constant companion, memory loss. And on the really tough mornings, I am Nurse Ratched, and my whole existence is for the purpose of exposing him as a forgetful, blind old man.

Which, if we're being honest, he is. But a properly medicated one.

HUMAN VS. ANIMAL

*Some of the relationships that are
impacted by being a caregiver become more
damaged than others. This includes animals.*

When we rescued our cat Maia in Maine over twelve years ago and brought her to our home in Connecticut, she promptly got out of the car and ran into the backyard. We didn't see her for an hour or two until she came back in to eat. That pretty much established her pattern as our cat for the next several years. She loved going outside and got very angry with us when we kept her in—which we did every night whether she liked it or not.

Snowy winters, rainy springs, humid summers, and windy falls didn't keep this cat in the house; I think we had one container of kitty litter for ten years she so rarely used the litter box. Then one recent winter, she stayed inside, curling up by radiators, or sprawled out on sunny spots in the kitchen, and sometimes hiding in small places like between the files on my bookcase that made her impossible to find. When we did, she'd just sit there looking at us as if to say, "Well, it took you long enough."

She was not a warm and fuzzy cat, but she was a clever and funny one. She did not like to snuggle. If I picked her up to hold her, within seconds she'd leap to the floor and run away. She would, however, eventually jump up on the couch or chair where Angelo and I were sitting to have her head scratched, sometimes even reaching out with her paw to remind us to do it. She wasn't always cuddly, but she was always smart, and we liked that in a cat. She was beautiful, too. We couldn't prove it, but we were pretty certain she had some Maine Coon in her. She was small but landed with the thud of a much larger animal as she jumped down from the kitchen counter when we caught her prowling for snacks. She had cool, green eyes, and every time I tried taking a picture of her beauty, the resulting image made her look like a demon. She's like the "two-faced" girlfriend from the Seinfeld episode who looks hideous in some lighting.

We've had other family members move in and out from time to time, and Maia appeared to be cool with that. Then, my dad moved in. At first, I was worried about her being underfoot. Since he couldn't see anything—except for his meals and CNN—one of my concerns was that he might trip over her. And since she was staying inside longer, she was around a lot. We installed a pet access panel in the basement door where we relocated her litter box—she was using it regularly now, so we actually had to add kitty litter to the shopping list. It seemed like she acclimated easily to that since she could still come and go as she pleased but continued to seek out the comfy spots in the house with more regularity.

All was well for the first six months of my dad's residency. Dad liked Maia, and Maia tolerated Dad. Occasionally, she would hop up to the side table next to the chair where he sat in the living room and poke at his sleeve to see if he would get up to let her out. When he didn't (because he didn't notice her or wasn't sure he could get the door open), she might just hang out next to him for a while. It seemed like an easy peace. Whew.

Then, one day, she pooped in his room. *What?!* I thought. *Must be some errant, one-time crazy accident!*

Until she peed on the rug next to his desk. And on the bathmat in his shower. And pooped again and again until she was finally relegated back to outside, where she took up a constant position on top of the grill. Through the spring and summer, it was like old times—she still preferred outside to in—but she came in to eat and sleep. In the basement. I just couldn't have her pooping inside the house and in particular, Dad's room!

As it got colder, we moved her inside again but kept her in the basement for the most part when we couldn't keep an eye on her. Then she peed in the front hall. This was getting serious, and Angelo and I began talking about vets, animal behavior, and unpleasant decisions as much as we talked about stress, lack of privacy, and wishing we could go to Italy. I am pretty sure Maia picked up on my frustration with her, too, because when I called her to come get her food, she would circle me warily and wait until I walked away before she began eating.

Her behavior, as we suspected, indicated a medical problem. To this day, I don't know exactly what it was because we decided to only treat her major symptoms: difficulty eating and a lack of grooming. And an overall antisocial attitude. We had to start fixing her food to make it easier to swallow by mashing it up and adding broth or a little bacon grease. I tried combing her, but she was now all-out mad at me and growled and swatted my hand away. Having to monitor her while I was also monitoring my dad doubled my stress. Was she upstairs? Did she go into my dad's room? Also, cleaning up pee and poop as a daily chore was more than I bargained for, no matter how necessary.

Because she was so ill, Angelo and I thought she was a goner—and sooner rather than later. But she hung on. She got thinner, more matted, and less friendly, but since we were keeping a pretty close eye on her, she rarely pooped in Dad's room anymore. (I say rarely because it continued happening when we let our guard down. In fact, she added the front hall rug to her favored poop spots.) She was eating and drinking water, which was amazing since the vet had suggested a tumor in her mouth, but it seemed to have disappeared. The stress on me increased as I became upset at how inhumane I was feeling toward the cat I had loved so much that she had her own chapter in my first book. I tried pet communication—looking deeply into her eyes and telepathically asking her what she needed. But she chose not to respond in kind.

Finally, Angelo and I confronted the decision to put her down. It took us three weeks from the moment we started the conversation to the morning we took her to the vet. Between her illness and her behavior, we decided she wasn't living her best life—it was time. That morning we gave her a big bowl of cream, and I tossed her a couple of bites of buttery scrambled eggs from my plate. She had taken to sitting right below my chair when I sat at the kitchen counter for breakfast. (I guess she wasn't *that* mad at me.) Fortunately, for me, Angelo had made The Appointment without consulting our shared calendar, and I had a class to teach that day. He took her in by himself and went back to pick her up by himself. We both buried her in the backyard near our first cat, Chloe. For company.

Since then, I think I see her out of the corner of my eye throughout the day. I save scraps of salmon after dinner, before suddenly realizing I don't need to. The patch of screen that she wouldn't stop clawing now brings a jolt of sadness rather than annoyance at one more thing I had to fix. Knowing it "was time" did not help us very much. It also didn't help that I kept thinking if Dad hadn't moved in, her departure wouldn't have been hastened. But I chase those thoughts away.

He missed her almost as much as we did.

YOU DON'T HAVE TO
DO CHRISTMAS CARDS

"Do you,' said I..."
—MARY SHELLEY, Frankenstein

I'm not mailing out Christmas cards this year.

One day I stared at the calendar on my computer screen and realized that the yellow squares for my new writing class overlapped with the light blue squares showing an end-of-year getaway I booked with my husband. A knot grew in the pit of my stomach; I have never done anything that blatantly erroneous before. Writing to the director to let her know of my mistake was one of the cringiest emails I've ever written and not because I haven't made mistakes before. Oh, yes. I have. This one, however, was an unabashed warning that I was slipping. But oddly, once I got past the sheer embarrassment of forgetting about a class I was supposed to teach, I realized that I also felt affirmed.

In just the span of a couple of years, my family and I suffered great loss and change. It began when my mother died of lung cancer. Given my dad's failing health and his reliance on my mother to care for him, my brother and I moved him to

Connecticut a few months later to live in my house. It would be good for him to be closer to my sister, also in Connecticut. She was battling her own cancer diagnosis and travel was out of the question; even the brief visits she made once he moved here were debilitating for her. A year later, she died. Her death was devastating, and I struggled dealing with a new layer of grief, even as I continued caring for dad. Then, a month later, I lost a good friend to a sudden heart attack.

Meanwhile, because conventional wisdom cautions caretakers to take time for themselves, I tried holding on to a small part of my own life. Not the part where I am wife, mother, grandmother, friend—babysitting, laundry, school pickups, grocery shopping, and maybe some cleaning—those roles fit in with some juggling. I can drag out a shower or trip to the pharmacy and grab twenty minutes of me-time easily. It was more challenging to claim my time as an author and writer. A *teaching* writer and author. I had plans for my second and third books. My writing practice needed some shoring up, and there were writing retreats to plan, and classes to pitch. It became clear, even to me, that I might be piling too much on my plate. About a year after my dad moved in, I realized that the bulk of my "work" was being a caretaker. But I didn't want to give up my career, so I found the places where I could squeeze it in. I thought I was handling it, even as colleagues described me as "overextended." I didn't want to believe it, but then I planned a trip to Kennebunkport, Maine on the day my next class was to start.

I hated realizing I had done that. Another time in my life, I might have—no, *probably* would have—tried convincing my husband to cut our trip short. So it was odd that I felt affirmed when I would typically be kicking myself for being such an idiot. However, in an unlikely turn of events, the same feeling of affirmation seemed to bring with it a clarity of priorities. We both needed this time away.

Being suffused with grief and sorrow brought me closer to discovering who I am as a person than almost any experience I've ever had. I think I've done okay navigating through the unimaginable pain that is loss, but starting to allow myself to be accepting of my mistakes or not getting everything done is something I typically haven't been that comfortable with. Other times of the year demand our attention, too, but at Christmas, the harsh light of expectation is disguised as colored bulbs ringing the front door or a sparkly star on the tree. The pressure to perform amid the surging currents of mourning is great. Grief takes up time and energy; it's not always immobilizing, but it always requires your attention.

So, I might not send out Christmas cards this year, but I can send out this message of affirmation to all those grappling with the vast layers of grief that the holidays bring: You are exactly where you need to be right now. Don't feel like baking gingerbread cookies? That's okay. Didn't get rolls of wrapping paper or spools of red and green ribbon? No problem. The gift of being open to the lessons of loss and what we can learn about ourselves is a more honest way to honor who you are as a person and a perfect gift to give yourself at Christmas.

THE PROPER CARE AND FEEDING OF YOUR CARETAKER

"Don't bite the hand that feeds you."
—ATTRIBUTED TO SAPPHO,
an early Greek influencer

When one is a caretaker for another human being, there is a tacit understanding that said caretaker will be available to the other human at any given time. This means lunches, appointments, errands, and light housekeeping. There is much the caretaker does in service for another that is done in person, even just being present in the same room. However, the caretaker needs a break from time to time. Well-intentioned family and friends will urge the caretaker to "Take time for *you!*" or "Don't forget to self-care!" These are legitimate suggestions, but the problem, of course, is that unless someone else is around to sub in for the caretaker, the caretaker isn't going anywhere. No matter how urgently he or she needs to flee.

For example, the following is a really generous offer: "I can come over and sit with your [father, mother, grandmother, sister, brother, cousin] for an hour if you need to get something done."

But it's a little vague. The need to get something done might come up at any time during the day or evening, and the offerer might be off having their own life. That is reasonable. Here's how to make that offer a little more solid: "I can come over on Friday at three for an hour if you need to run out and get some errands done." Now, the caretaker can respond with something like: "We have Mah-jongg at three on Friday, but I'd love to run out to the grocery at one." Definite days and times give the caretaker something to plan on.

One day I was complaining to my friend David about my urgent need for a haircut and a general all-around lack of time. He listened patiently while I vented, and then he suggested I make a wish list. (Thank God he didn't offer to cut my hair.)

"Why? To give myself more to do?" I shot back.

He ignored that. "Why not write down everything that would make your life easier, no matter how unlikely it sounds."

"That will just make me sound whiny," I whined.

"No, it won't. It might help you get a clear idea of what would actually be helpful to you as opposed to simply accepting offers of help that don't really do anything. It doesn't do you any good to accept an offer that isn't what you need—then you're just helping your friend feel better. Plus, it might be fun to give your imagination a whirl and wish for a foot massage by Brad Pitt. It will never happen, but a girl can dream."

As reasonable as he sounded, the idea fluttered away as I stopped at the pharmacy to pick up a prescription and grab some almond milk at the market on the way home. Later, though, when I thought about it, I realized stress does tend to dampen the imagination. It might be fun to take my mind off the week's To-Do list and see if I could come up with a For-Me list.

Turns out, David was right. Not only was it fun to indulge in my wildest dreams, but creating a list actually helped clarify some real needs I had been overlooking. And knowing exactly what I needed helped me take care of it, whether or not someone is offering to help. Unless it's that foot massage thing. That I'll let Brad Pitt take care of.

My Wish List

- Sometimes I wish I could open the fridge and have the evening meal ready to pop in the oven.
- I wish I knew someone who could manage the mountain of paperwork that comes along with old age. Medicare, insurance, doctors, prescriptions—piles are accumulating in my office. This person could also make all the phone calls that accompany the paperwork.
- I wish I could spend a weekend alone in a hotel with a pillow-top mattress, room service, wi-fi, and an electrical outlet right next to the bed. Oh, and a bottle of Old Vine Zin would be a nice touch.
- I wish that, when I found I had an afternoon free, I had a gift card for a pedicure, a haircut, the movies, or a bookstore so I would know what to do with my unexpected free time.
- I wish someone would come over and tell me what to do with my garden. (This really doesn't have to do with being a caretaker, but I really need help with my garden. It's a *wish* list after all.)
- Occasionally, especially on high-maintenance days, it would be nice to get a quick, supportive text, email, or voicemail. Such a message is a nice little pick-me-up especially when I can't get to the phone. An actual card in the mail is like winning the lottery.
- And speaking of winning the lottery, I wish I could put an in-law addition onto my house so my dad could have his own "quarters" rather than just live in my remodeled dining room.
- I wish my dad's doctors would be the ones who decide his medical care and not the insurance companies.
- It might be kind of nice if that foot massage could be arranged. It doesn't even have to be Brad Pitt. I'd be okay with my husband providing it. In Amalfi, Italy.

DOCTOR'S ORDERS

"Take two aspirin and call me in the morning."
—Long-standing doctor joke

Every three months or so, Dad and I would head out for another round of doctor's appointments. He had six of them: a primary care doctor (his third in two years), a diabetes doc, a cardiologist, an ophthalmologist, a neurologist, and a podiatrist. Oh, and a dentist. Seven. They all wanted him to have a check-up appointment, even though we both knew nothing was going to get "better." At any given appointment and with any of the above seven docs, meds got adjusted, strategies got changed, or directives were mandated. Sometimes all three.

Oh, and he had a therapist. Eight.

We would leave each appointment with anything from a reminder not to use too much salt (typically ignored) to a whole new scale from which to dose his three-times-a-day insulin. Obviously, none of these doctors talked to each other, so it was up to me to manage all the medical advice and information and distill it in a way that made sense to our daily routine. Actually, two of the docs worked in the same medical group, but they couldn't even manage to synchronize the appointment schedule (the last time each office booked his next appointment within an hour of the other on the same day). They could hardly be expected to know whether one doctor's advice would conflict with the other one.

And it's not really a conflict in information. I'm sure each doctor was confident in the knowledge that they dispensed was accurate, helpful, and even life-saving advice to my dad. It's just that, if I were to carefully observe each new strategy that was given to us, I'd need an extra ten hours in the day to make it all work. And every three months, it would all change again. Each doctor looked at this twenty-minute snapshot of Dad's life and made a determination about what the following three months should look like. If I was ever so bold to interject any comments, I often—not always, but often enough to make me hesitant—get one of those looks that clearly told me I wasn't the medical professional and maybe I was just complaining a little.

Of course, all of the above goes out the window if there is a hospitalization, which, of course, there was. Dad, a little impatient with waiting for us to get the car ready to go out to dinner, decided to head outside to the driveway on his own. I saw him come out the door and I motioned to Angelo, who was clearing the back seat, that Dad was on the move. Before either of us could react—down he went. Angelo got to him first and tried to help him upright.

He groaned when he had to move his leg, so we had him sit for a bit. When he put the slightest amount of weight on his foot, he cried out in pain. He waved us off, though, insisting he would feel better once we got going. He didn't want to be the reason we were delayed; it was the anniversary of the day of my sister's death, and we were on our way to meet her husband and son at her favorite restaurant. We got him into the car using his rollator (a walker and seat combined), and off we went. During dinner we could see he was clearly in pain, it was *not* getting better. We stopped at the ER on the way home. Broken ankle.

No one could believe he had gone so long without attention. (But then, no one knew how much Dad had waited to have his favorite scallops dish.)

They "fixed" it and told me he'd probably go home in a day or two. But I knew better; Medicare won't cover any rehab he might need unless he spends three nights in the hospital. And even though we arrived at ten on a Wednesday night, and they were literally working on his ankle, he wasn't "admitted," so his first night wouldn't be until Thursday at midnight. That worked out okay because the surgeon who came in to examine him said he wasn't crazy about the first "reduction" that had been done on the ankle. The bones were still crooked so he would need surgery and another day or two for recovery. Dad was definitely in for a hospital stay.

It's a real Catch-22, this hospital stay thing. On the one hand, we needed him to stay in order to be eligible in case he needed additional coverage. On the other hand, all our meticulous care of him, including diet, medications, and general welfare, were then under a most institutional schedule.

The Dexcom continuous glucose monitoring device was ignored; they had their own scale for insulin injections. Their scale was completely different, meant for a Type 2 diabetic— no insulin unless his blood sugar read 150. But he was a Type 1 diabetic, and his need for insulin began when his blood sugar read sixty if he was about to have a meal. As handy as this device is for a diabetic, the hospital couldn't have cared less. I could continue monitoring it while he was at the hospital through an app for family members to be able to keep up with the readings, but that rendered me helpless as I sat at home and could only watch his blood sugar shoot up to 400 or drop to 50.

It took several pleadings from me to change the insulin injections to the scale he came in with, and I had to call his endocrinologist for backup. "Just make sure they know he doesn't have any insulin in his body," she told me. Right. I'll just tell all the medical professionals how to do their job. They love that.

Because his doctor wasn't going to go in and do it. It used to be that when you chose a hospital, you had to make sure that your doctor had "privileges" there. Now, doctors don't even come into the hospital at all to see their patients; there's a *hospitalist* for that. All the information sitting in your chart that specifically pertains to you is all for naught because now the hospitalist, who doesn't know you or your dad from Adam, is in charge.

With an elder, a family member or friend *has* to be present at almost every interaction, particularly if that elder can't remember to insist on their own individual care. Meals, meds, instructions—it's overwhelming and confusing. At least this elder—my dad—gave in to the inevitable, "They have to do everything their way, so why fight it?"

During shift change one afternoon, I overheard the departing nurse in the hallway tell the arriving one, "This family is hyper-vigilant," with a quick nod to Dad's room. I happened to be standing in the doorway and caught the comment, so I said, not so much under my breath, "No, just regular vigilant." I didn't raise my voice or stomp my feet, but, yes, I was vigilant, or, perhaps a better word: an advocate.

WORK LIKE IT'S A REAL JOB

*"Didn't anyone tell you it was
going to be a full-time job?"*
—A nurse at yet another doctor's office
while making an appointment for my dad.

One of the best and worst things anyone ever said to me was that the care I was giving my dad would cost about $112,000 a year from a professional. I'm a professional. Just not the credentialed home-aide kind. Although I'm pretty sure I'm getting the equivalent of a master's degree in geriatric home care.

There are little ironies that show up all throughout taking in an elder parent or loved one (LO) and giving them the best care possible. Here's one: The attention the LO is getting will probably make them resentful at some point. This is reasonable. However, they very well might take out that resentment on the caregiver—you. They might say mean or sarcastic things. Thank-yous will be few and far between, and it won't seem at all that the dedication you are demonstrating is appreciated. The behavior and attitude of the LO is not commensurate with what you've given up in order to take care of them.

You understand this, of course, because you are aware of the breadth of this person's life. It is easy to imagine how difficult and even humiliating it must be to have someone fix all your meals or clean up your bathroom accidents. You will have many more conversations about shit than you ever imagined having with your LO. Or anyone. Even so, this unpleasant behavior will hurt, for many reasons but mainly because of the close family relationship that led you to bring your LO into your home in the first place. It will make you think that it might be better for everyone to have the LO live in another place, an assisted living or other residential care facility.

That's another irony: Even if it seems like it might be better for everyone's mental health for your LO to live in a professional facility, it will be hard to give up the care of them.

The professional staff at such places are (hopefully) trained to deal with the kind of cranky and resentful behavior that results from a once independent and functioning adult having to give over his or her care to others. But, the care that the LO receives at a commercial facility won't be nearly as individualized or vigilant as the care you are providing and, therefore, the very care and understanding is exactly the opposite of the kind that your LO will get at a professional facility. Not to condemn commercial residences, but there, your loved one is a job. In your home, they are your life.

The work that you are doing to keep your LO safe, happy, and alive *is* a full-time job. Particularly if they are living in your home. Again, this is not to say that caregivers who have parents or family members already living in a professional setting aren't stressed out—they are. Much of that stress comes from wondering what's happening when you aren't there to keep an eye on things.

But that's a whole other chapter.

"CAN I HELP?"

"We are all here on earth to help others;
what on earth the others are here for I don't know."
—W. H. AUDEN

Dad often volunteers to help me with routine household chores. For example, when I've come in from the grocery, he'll say, "Need anything brought in?" Or when I lug his laundry out of his room and head to the basement stairs, he'll offer, "Need a hand with that?" The problem, of course, is that he can do none of that. His offers simultaneously frustrate me and pierce my heart.

Dad has always been a "do-er," a problem solver. Like most men, I guess, and many women, he saw every problem as an opportunity to fix and make things better. He was always volunteering his time, Mom's time, and our time, for community activities. Once we kids dropped out of his recruitment net, he and Mom continued throughout our childhood and into their retirement.

After Mom and Dad moved to Florida, they worked on houses for Habitat for Humanity and served at homeless shelters. Dad created a group of like-minded activists, called their team "Peace by Piece" and promoted integrating a conflict resolution curriculum in the Sarasota public schools. He joined others from his church to initiate SURE, an action-based organization to hold elected officials accountable to the needs of the disadvantaged communities in Sarasota. One of his proudest problem-solving achievements was to help establish a branch of the public library in an underserved area of town.

As he got older, blindness limited his activity but not his desire to help. He could only be involved in the things that Mom was willing to drive him to or where he could find a friend with whom he could hitch a ride. When that started slowing down, he still attended the bi-weekly CEO informational meetings in their retirement facility, so he could stay apprised of any matters that might need attention. His attention. The times that I attended with him, I was directed to take notes; he often dozed off.

Right before he fell and was in a coma for ten days, Dad had declined to be almost non-communicative. He listened to his books on tape, ate his meals, and watched Rachel Maddow every night, but just didn't seem to be there. My own diagnosis was that he couldn't do anything to help anyone anymore, primarily Mom, so he just checked out. She herself had become visibly impatient with him, and watching the two of them was increasingly difficult—my parents seemed like they just didn't care anymore, about each other or themselves.

Then, the fall and the coma. We were at his side nearly 24/7 throughout his hospitalization, the removal of his ventilator, and his miraculous recovery. When he returned home—at least to the rehab wing of their building—no one was more shocked that he was still alive than he was, except maybe Mom. He became much more responsive than after the previous year or so. I think all the attention he was getting helped—and not so much because he was being paid attention to, but because he was being given something to do. He had a job, a purpose. He could help!

Whenever any of us kids had a major life experience come up—going to college, buying a house, raising a child—Dad had a spreadsheet for it. Or a Pro/Con worksheet. Or a book to read by the latest expert. He attacked the schedules and exercises from the occupational and physical therapists with the same gusto. Was there a worksheet? Great. Did he have to figure out a plan? Perfect. Richard would quiz him on the week's current events during their weekly Sunday night phone call. He appeared to be more engaged and aware than he was before the coma. I think it was because he had something to fix. Himself.

Then he moved in with us. There really wasn't that much to do, and it became increasingly clear that he wasn't going to improve. I knew allowing him to do as much as he was able was beneficial, but there was a line between allowing and enabling. I couldn't keep allowing him to pour his own cereal in the morning if it meant that half the time it would spill out on the floor. And not because cleaning up cereal from the floor is such a big deal, but the combination of his spilling, my cleaning, and his not being able to do anything about it set off a day's worth of frustration and anger that was better off avoided. Angelo and I *wanted* him to do more for himself, but it became too much more work for us.

Susie used to come over to "help," but she mostly slept in the guest room upstairs or on the couch in the living room—next to Dad sleeping in his chair. One night, at dinner, she got some terrible news—recent bloodwork showed she needed more tests, and she was having an argument with her husband about having to schedule them at a time when he had other plans. As she teared up, she was having trouble with the food on her plate—it was slipping about and she couldn't manage it—she dropped her hands in her lap and simply gave up. Dad, sitting next to her, quietly pulled her plate over near him and cut up the grilled sausage and roasted potatoes for her and then, just as quietly, pushed it back toward her. He still had some help left in him.

Every morning at breakfast, Dad shares what he dreamed the night before. It usually starts out, "I had the weirdest dreams last night . . ." and then he'll describe being at a conference with former colleagues or some other work-related scenario. They are often about Mom, too, as in seeing her sitting across the room from him or even lying in bed with him. When she's sitting, she's at the table in his room across from the bed. He tries talking to her, but he can't always understand her. He can always see her, though. One morning, he complained that she was sleeping on the side of the bed from which he usually gets up and he couldn't go to the bathroom because she was in the way!

If it's not about Mom, he dreams of doing stuff. Hard and challenging stuff. One night he's in the mountains using heavy machinery to take down trees and load logs onto trucks to clear a path. Or he's having to drive home through a thick fog at night because he has to go to a friend's house to help him. Another night he's living in New York City, as he always dreamed of, visiting the Russian Tea Room, and going to concerts. He dreams he's capable and strong and independent—and helpful.

One of the most intense dreams was that Mom had come back. He didn't know how it happened, but there she was right in front of him. She had come back, and instead of driving off to Maine together or going out to dinner, in his dream, he had to assemble a team of professionals to verify it was her and announce her return. He knew he needed a minister—their old friend Paul—and their lawyer, and a doctor. He had to decide which friend to contact and if Mom would like who he chose. The dream faded away as dreams usually do without any resolution to the problem: how to announce to the world that Mom was back. He woke up frustrated because he still had work to do.

He just wants to help.

SUSAN DALE EASTMAN ALLISON

Doolittle Funeral Services, Inc.
Susan Dale Eastman Allison Obituary
June 12, 1961 ~ May 15, 2018 (Age 56)

Susan Allison, 56, is the first Poet Laureate of Middletown, Connecticut. She was born in Derby, Connecticut, and raised in Louisville, Kentucky. She attended Wesleyan University in Middletown and, after a year of mountain climbing and traveling through East Africa, she graduated in 1985 with a BA in African Studies.

Shortly after graduation, she opened an old and rare bookshop, Ibis Books & Gallery, on Rapallo Avenue in Middletown's North End. The shop was transformed in 1991 into NEAR, Inc. and the Buttonwood Tree, an arts and cultural performance space now on Main Street, which continues to be a hub of artistic and cultural activity. Susan's second book of poetry was published by Antrim House Books in 2009. Annie Dillard calls her second book of poetry, *Down by the Riverside Ways*, "the work of a talented poet." Rennie McQuilken, Connecticut's Poet Laureate and publisher, says, "Susan Allison has done for Middletown, Connecticut, what

Williams did for Paterson, New Jersey: she has seen past its pedestrian surface to its mythical underpinnings. She has written a book whose passion, honesty, and visceral style make it an important contribution to the world of poetry." Susan has two poetry books soon to be published by Ibis Books: *Poet Laureate of Middletown Proclaimed and Provoked* and *Be Full*.

Susan is survived by her husband Stephan, and son John, father Warren Eastman, sister Cynthia Eastman, her husband Angelo Farenga and their children Christopher Willis; Annie Musso and husband Anthony and son Luca; Justine Pilar and husband Adam and children Madeline and Aiden. Her brother Richard Eastman; her brother-in-law Fredrick Allison, sisters-in-law Gretchen Shannon and husband Terrence and children Jesse and Sarah, and Anne Brown and husband Steuart and daughter Allie and husband Joshua. Susan was predeceased by her mother Patricia Russell Eastman.

A public celebration of Susan's life will take place on June 16, beginning at 5:30 p.m. at the Community Health Center, Main St., Middletown.

In lieu of flowers, donations can be made to the Susan D. E. Allison Fund, Community Foundation of Middlesex County, 49 Main St., Middletown, CT 06457.

THE DAY HE DIES

"Old age should burn and rave at close of day."
—DYLAN THOMAS

One day I realized that the cozy bedroom we created out of our dining room off of our kitchen could very well be the place my dad dies. Since then, I've imagined that day over a thousand times. If you haven't considered what it will be like when the parent you've moved into your home dies, it might hit you one day when you least expect it. For me, it was a few months after Dad moved in. There wasn't an incident—no fall or spill or sudden confusion. I think it was just a typical day, and I was walking through the kitchen and happened to look in on him sitting at his table—as usual. A sudden flash like a premonition appeared in my head: One day my dad will die here in my home. My home will be the place he dies. It was sad and a little creepy all at once. I honestly don't recall thinking about that when we moved him; we didn't really think through lots of situations at all. All we knew was that he couldn't stay where he was.

Since that day, I've thought about it a lot. I don't have to remind you that there are several essays in this very book that detail those (sometimes morbid) thoughts. I believe he deserves to die in his sleep; experience tells me it will be more problematic than that. Another fall, perhaps during one of the several times he gets up at night to pee. Maybe a diabetic issue, like low blood sugar or an accidental incorrect insulin injection. Whatever it will be, it will probably require dealing with more doctors who don't believe he is a Type 1 diabetic, or a facility that can't give him the accommodations he needs, or adding two or three more appointments each week, like having to go to the Wound Clinic after the surgery on his ankle didn't heal properly.

No, he won't go out with a whimper, but a bang. It will be more energy, more time, and more management of his already burdensome oversight. It will be a case that doesn't fit into any typical situations, but one that requires more . . . something. He'll play it down, but it will require even more attention, from other family members or medical personnel. All of which will serve to make him more cranky, more difficult to deal with and impossible to reason with.

He already feels like a burden, and whatever his future demise will entail, it will only make it worse. The night he was to be discharged from the hospital to the skilled nursing facility for his broken ankle, he sat grumpily in his hospital bed, legs splayed out across the bed with the hospital gown not doing a great job of providing modesty. As I sat with him to keep him company through the transition, he blatantly accused me of having something to do with his fall down the stairs which resulted in the injury.

I don't want to find him dead in his bed one morning. I mean—I do, and I don't. He's miserable, and a quiet and simple end to his well-lived life would be earned. I just don't want to be the one to discover that it has finally happened.

As much as I've anticipated—and if we're being honest, hoped for—his passing, I am pretty sure I will be devastated when it does happen. Unless I go first—which is a whole other conversation. My dad has lived with us for about three years longer than any of us ever expected, including himself, I suspect. Who knows how much longer he will hang on, defying conventional medical wisdom. His two brothers—both in better shape than he—have both passed. Years ago. His father went to live with his oldest son for about a year before he died—in his sleep at the age of ninety—and he didn't have half the medical complications that Dad has.

Ten years ago, his diabetes was supposed to kill him. It hasn't. Five years ago, a concussion and resulting coma should have been the end of him (I think my Mom was pretty sure it would be) but instead he came out of it more alert and competent than before. Even the recent broken ankle, and its subsequent reset, resulted in the surgeon warning us about the danger of such a procedure because even a non-invasive one that required anesthesia could cause damage to his already complex medical status. Not only did he survive that, but an additional surgery, invasive this time, where the bone was reset with twelve pins and two metal plates. It seems like he's just not ready to go, doesn't it?

And yet, every single day, I have to be ready for how his death is going to happen because this is not a man who is going to go quietly into that good night.

THE DARK SIDE

"That which does not kill us, makes us stronger."
—NIETZSCHE
A positive quote on dark times

"What doesn't kill me might make me kill you."
—INTERNET MEME
A more realistic quote on dark times

One night, I had a dream where my brother and I were concocting a plan to kill our father. It wasn't a terribly graphic dream with blood and guts and sirens. It was actually kind of benign, having to do with placing different types of cables and power cords in his room. And not to strangle or electrocute—just to place them there. The dream ended with us agreeing to use the black cable instead of the white one, and the outcome of the decision was not evident. It's likely that even in my dream state, there wasn't a clearer plan of action because I didn't really want to kill my father. I'm pretty sure my brother didn't want to either. But do I wake up each morning wondering if he's survived the night? Yep.

Sometimes, when you think that you can't wait for things to get better, you realize better means someone has to be dead.

One evening, I was at my neighbor Claire's house seeking support and empathy from her and another neighbor, Michelle. And wine. I was also seeking wine. And chocolate. I got all of it. Michelle had to leave early, and as she stood at the door, she turned back to me and said sympathetically, "I hope things get better for you."

From the fridge, replenishing our wine, Claire said bluntly, "Better is loss." Michelle cringed a little as she pulled on her gloves for the walk back across the street to the less brusque safety of her own house, but it made me think for a minute. She was right. Better means loss.

Sounds pretty harsh, I know, but if you think about it, it's the truth. At the time, the only way my life was going to change was if my dad died or suffered a debilitating illness or injury and had to be hospitalized. And we all know hospitalization equals death for many elders with health issues.

If no one was looking, I bet that if I asked for a show of hands to see how many caregivers wake up each morning wondering if their caregivee is dead, I don't think mine would be the only one up in the air. It's a fact of life that old people die eventually, so it's not outrageous or mean to consider what life will be like "after." But after several years of 24/7 care from those of us who are actually on the retirement side of aging, a few years can seem like an eternity. The constant daily vigilance necessary to care for an aging loved one is enormously stressful. The parents in our care probably have some other issues that require extra attention and supervision, like dementia, diseases, debilitation, etc. They wouldn't be in our care otherwise, would they? They'd be playing canasta in Florida or watering their lawns in Arizona, and we'd see them at Christmas and Facetime with them on birthdays and other holidays.

We care for our parents because of either health or financial limitations. Both of which create an extra burden for caregivers. We give up current employment or add to it. There's really nothing about making the decision to become a caregiver that says, "This will be rewarding!" and yet, that's what almost every single person to whom you report your new situation will say to you:

"Oh, that's such a great opportunity for you!"

"They took care of us, it's our turn to take care of them!"

"You'll never regret spending this time with your mother (or father)."

"Well, that's life!"

It will make you want to slap someone. I know I wanted to. (I didn't, just to clarify.)

It was important for me to acknowledge this dark side of my understanding of what it was like to care for my father. We basically turned over our lives to tend to his. My husband gave up his own retirement plan to have my father in our home. I gave up pursuing my second career as a (paid) writer in order to be available 24/7 to my father's needs—which are many, constant, and multiplying. I'm sorry—this was not a rewarding journey for us, and if I'm honest (and I believe that I have been), I didn't make the decision thinking he would actually live as long as he did.

He had Type 1 diabetes for over forty years. He survived a head trauma and a 10-day coma, he has a heart pacer, and he's legally blind. On the emotional side, he lost his wife of sixty years to a fast-moving lung cancer diagnosis, and a year later, his youngest daughter—also to cancer. All of which has combined to make him angry, sad, frustrated, paranoid, and miserable. And alive to endure it. When he ended up in the ER dehydrated and with a case of pneumonia, they sent him home the next day with some antibiotics!

My husband and I couldn't make spontaneous plans to go out to dinner, treat ourselves to a shopping trip a couple of towns over, or go away for the weekend. We had limited resources for bringing in care for the rare outing, but Dad resented it so much—he didn't think he needed it—it was easier to just skip it and eat at home or order online or put off our getaway for later.

You know, when things were better.

DO MORE?

"More, more, more . . ."
—THE ANDREA TRUE CONNECTION

M y writing classes often include returning students, so there
is some built-in familiarity in addition to creating a community of trust when beginning a new class. It is in that context
that I shared with all the students in a new course—a couple
of new ones, a couple of returnees—one of the latest debacles
I experienced as a caregiver for my eighty-nine-year-old dad.

That very morning, his most recent aide showed up and
had to "talk to me." Even though it had only been her second
day, she couldn't return. Apparently, she had a reaction to some
. . . *thing* in my home, and it had triggered her respiratory
ailments, and as much as she enjoyed her first (and only) day,
she had to quit.

One of the repeat students asked further about the situation, and I shared a little more about the frustration and
exhaustion I had been feeling before dropping my personal
woes and moving on to the actual content of the class. As
we ended, one of the new students—a woman—said she had
taken care of her mother for twenty-five years. I think I nearly

dropped my teeth. She added, "I probably shouldn't tell you this, but the one thing my husband and I both agreed on after she died was that we wished we could have done more." I nearly snorted in disbelief. She understood that I probably didn't feel that way now, but she thought she'd share that with me. I was, uncharacteristically, speechless.

I drove home with one thought ping-ponging around my brain: how could I possibly do *more*?

In three years, I lost my mom, my sister, my freedom, my husband's retirement plans, our privacy, my income, my outside activities, my sleep pattern, my generally sunny disposition, and honestly, my dad. At eighty-nine, he had suffered similar losses and had fewer resources with which to deal with them, which made him grow increasingly unhappy and angry. He was not able to engage with us in a comfortable and stress-free way so we could help him but was suspicious and anxious. He lashed out at both Angelo and me with regularity and, one time, I remember vividly his scathing glare when I told him I would be upstairs in my office to get some work done. The reason? After the visiting nurse finished dressing his still-open wound from the ankle surgery eight months earlier, Angelo and I spoke privately to her in the kitchen about finding additional services in order to continue to care for him in our home. She promised she'd get back to us and I went back into his room to help him use the remote to his TV. There, on his face, was the familiar tight-lipped grimace that indicated his suspicion that we were talking about him. Which, of course, we were.

But only to find some help to shore up the areas where we were falling short. We were nearly at our limit even as we understood that there was literally no end in sight. And to hear the woman in class express that she wished she could have done more—well, I simply couldn't believe my ears.

But the thought kept bouncing around. I couldn't let go of trying to understand how anyone could do more. More what?

More time spent driving to doctors and drugstores; taking him to see his friends, or just getting out for a change of scenery? More meals made, more loads of laundry folded, more cleaning up after him? More of my own life—and Angelo's—given up to tend to his increasing needs? More letting go of time spent with my children and grandchildren, which was the whole reason I decided to forgo a real job and devote time to developing a writing career, which I had to abandon as soon as I started?

It was very difficult for me to see where I could be doing more. And, in fact, it took my imagining Dad's death to be able to bring in another lens through which to look. It took a few days, but eventually, I began seeing where I might be able to do more.

I wish I could be more patient; less impatient. I wish I wasn't so quick to react. I wish there were more times I could keep my tongue in check; to keep from being annoyed or arguing with him. I knew he was frustrated with his diminished abilities, even though most of the time he wasn't really accepting of them and thought he could still care for himself. He couldn't. I wish I had more resources, more money, and more help in order to have made him feel comfortable and safe. And loved.

Of course, I couldn't *make* him feel safe, cared for, and loved. He insisted that he was a burden at the same time we tried to assure him otherwise, even as the demand for more attention and help to his needs increased. He deserved to feel safe and loved. He didn't need to hear my impatient sighs or frustrated comments when I had to bend down on sixty-two-year-old knees to sponge up the scrambled eggs or cherry Jell-O from the floor beneath his chair in the kitchen. He didn't deserve to feel as though he was in the way when I complained about not being able to attend a workshop or meeting because someone had to stay home with him.

What he deserved was to die peacefully in his sleep. To have a nice meal—maybe Fettuccine Alfredo, a Würzburger

Hofbräu beer, and, for dessert, a small scoop of mocha ice cream with dark chocolate chips. Then he could watch Rachel Maddow skewer Trump, take out his teeth, put on his pajamas, climb into bed, and fall asleep. And not wake up in the morning. I could only imagine my sadness if that happened, but he was miserable and unhappy and he missed my mom. There was little left for him in this world.

One morning, over breakfast, Dad told me about a dream he had. He was waiting in a line, dressed in some sort of robe and Mom was there, but not there, as it happens in dreams. He understood he was waiting to get into Heaven and he could see around him people who probably shouldn't have been in that line. (Ever judgmental, even in his dreams.) Then, he got through the line, and he finally found her. They were back together again.

I don't know how I could do more than that.

AMAZON SEARCH HISTORY—
SANDWICH GENERATION VERSION

"If you haven't found it yet, keep looking."
—STEVE JOBS

March
Caregiver guidebooks
Dri-Nite waterproof mattress protector—twin-size
DentuCreme-secure hold-bulk
Hearing aid batteries
Bedtime story books, ages 5–7 years old
Herbal Tea, Matcha Positive Energy 2.02 oz. (Pack of 12)

May
Disinfecting wipes
Toddler wipes
Safety Time Audio baby monitor (2)

September
Back to school supplies, ages 5–7
Depends Guards for Men—worry-free to prevent leaks
Neptune Waterproof Chair Protector Pads
Home video cameras multi-pack

Smells Begone Odor Eliminator Gel Beads, Air Freshener
for bathrooms, bedrooms, kitchens

December
LEGO anything
Easy button extra thick flannel shirts, men
Adult Coloring Book: Stress-Relieving Animal Designs
Noise-canceling headphones, adults
Noise-canceling headphones, kids
CBD oil for stress

January
Depends briefs Size Medium—Real fit Maximum
absorbency—subscribe and save!
GoodSense Polyethylene Glycol 3350 Powder for
Constipation Relief, 17.9 Ounce
Flushable wipes
Joke books for kids
Meditation chimes

February
Memory aids for adults
Small Dry Erase Whiteboard—Desktop Portable mini
To Do List for Office, Home, School.
Dry erase markers
Nighty-Night Natural Children's Sleep Tablet with
Melatonin, Cherry Flavor, 30 Chewable Tablets

April
CBD edibles
Lindt chocolate, bulk

July
Drive Medical Four-Wheel Rollator with Fold Up

Removable Back Support
Easy Readers books, first grade
Portable pill containers
125 Count Jell-O Shot Soufflé Cups and Lids,
    1-ounce, Translucent

September
SecureMe Bed Rail for Seniors, Adjustable Bed Assist Rail
    Handle, and Fall Prevention Safety
Minion nightlight
Motion sensor nightlights
YumYum Applesauce pouches, (48 pouches), Healthy
Snacks, Great for Lunches or mixing with medications

December
Wine-any size
Mom Juice Cup—12 oz. Stainless Steel Stemless Insulated
    Wine Tumbler Cup

January
Stay Busy Interactive Bead activity set. Over 20,000 beads!
Hours of Fun! 4+
Books on Dementia
*The 36-Hour Day: A Family Guide to Caring for
    People Who Have Alzheimer's Disease, Related
    Dementias, and Memory Loss*

March
Automatic pill dispenser
CBD anything

June
Drive Medical Blue Streak Wheelchair with Flip Back
    Arms, Swing Away Footrests

Able Life Auto Assist Grab Bar—Vehicle Support Handle
& Standing Mobility Aid
Stress relief adults
Fuck It! Button—Features ten outrageously funny Fuck It
phrases with crazy background sound effects

August
Shark Backpack for School, with Adjustable, Padded Straps
SeeMe-PeeMe—2 Pc. 32 Ounce Deluxe Male Urinal Glow
in the Dark Incontinence Pee Bottle
Prime Video subscription
Mellow Out Anxiety relief essential oils—stress relief on the
go-therapeutic grade

SOMEBODY

"I'm Nobody! Who are you?
Are you—Nobody—too?
Then there's a pair of us!

How dreary—to be—Somebody! . . . *"*
—EMILY DICKINSON
A well-known recluse

Somebody should . . . make an appointment to get the snow tires on.

Somebody should . . . make sure that the arrangements to meet Cousin Charlie are all set.

Somebody should . . . see to getting the Christmas cards done. Do "we" have the list from last year?

Somebody should . . . call the bank and try to get that charge refunded.

I think somebody told me that Christopher was starting his new job on Monday.

Who's Somebody? It's me. I'm Somebody.

Nothing erases a person's efforts at caregiving more than being referred to as "somebody." It's not like my dad doesn't realize who is doing all these tasks and errands—is it? Is it part of the dementia or just denial that keeps him from acknowledging all the work I do in service to his needs? It's not like there's anyone else around doing these things. Angelo maybe, and sometimes Christopher. Occasionally Richard when he flies in for a couple of weeks. But mostly, it's me who's given up my time and career to keep him alive and in reasonably good health.

One day, as I was on my hands and knees scrubbing the bathroom floor for the umpteenth time that week, Dad nearly tripped over me as he tried to get in. I hadn't heard him and quickly alerted him to the fact that I was there. "I'm just doing a little tidying," I said from the floor.

"*Urg* . . . tha . . . *umm* . . . *grp* . . . ." he grunted. I think it was "thank you," but it was hard to make out.

I don't do this for the glory, but some recognition might be nice once in a while. From anybody.

HITLER'S DAUGHTER

"It's a blessing and a curse."
—ADRIAN MONK

I think I'm the only living person in the world who isn't grateful to be taking care of her eighty-nine-year-old father in her home. The truth is, he shouldn't even be alive, considering the Type 1 diabetes, legal blindness, and heart pacer. He has endured traumatic brain injury as a result of a fall and the ensuing ten-day coma and managed a broken ankle and a prolonged stay in a skilled nursing facility. After that? He was hospitalized for pneumonia, but he was discharged after only one day and sent home with antibiotics. Which he took without any side effects, except for curing him. He suffered two profound losses in recent years—his wife and his "favorite daughter."

Any one of the above-mentioned calamities should have killed him; that he survived at all is one of the hardest things to comprehend. Not because I marvel at his ability to cheat death, but because it makes me a person who thinks her father should be dead. Even worse than those terrible thoughts is the one where I don't want to be my dad's caretaker anymore. My life feels cursed. What is wrong with me? Was I someone terrible in my former life? Was I patient zero for the Black Death? Did I hold the door open for John Wilkes Booth at Ford's Theater? Was I Hitler's secret daughter?

Practically since the day my mom died, I have been providing 24/7 care for my dad. I think the hardest thing about caring for a parent is when their personality changes from what you've known for most of your life. My father, who was always the patient, funny, giving, community activist, became a paranoid, sarcastic, insulting old man. He doesn't appear grateful for any of the care he receives; in fact, he seems to become more resentful of it with each passing day.

He complains daily that he can't button his shirt, put in his hearing aids, or Velcro his shoes—all because he can't see. It is also because of his diminished cognitive abilities, but he can't help but blame almost everyone and everything else.

When he first moved in, we brought in educators from the Bureau of Blind Services to help him acclimate to his new surroundings. He was given strategies, exercises, tips, and support to help him with his failing eyesight. But does he do or remember any of them? No. And if I remind him, I'm the problem. One day, he started asking me to bring back the blind counselors, to "help" him, but I know how that will end. He has no learning curve anymore, but he can't know or understand that. Of course, finding out if he is still eligible for services would be one more thing I have to schedule and make time for, after which he will complain about the difficulty and then not remember to do any of the techniques anyway. Besides the actual direct care, there is all the paperwork, phone calls, scheduling, re-scheduling, etc. that takes time and energy away from anything I want to be doing for my own life. Which he is aware of and also makes him angry, but he is unable to direct that anger anywhere but, ironically, at me.

I try to not engage with his resentment and anger, but I can't help myself sometimes. My patience is at a negative level and there are some days I can't shut the fuck up. When the visiting nurse came to bandage the wound from his broken ankle (oh, right—he has an eight-month-old open wound that requires a visit to the wound clinic every two weeks and a visit from the nurse three times a week), he joked that he almost fell the other day (because falling is so hilarious). She smiled at him and said, "Oh we wouldn't want that!" and I couldn't help but add, "Because I don't have enough to do already." The thing about that particular sarcastic quip is that I actually thought about it first, decided it wouldn't be necessary, and then said it anyway. He's oh-so funny and charming with the visiting nurses but can barely choke out a thank you when I fix him some cinnamon toast because his blood sugar is dropping a little.

They call him "cute" and "adorable" and he gets more *awwws* than a clumsy puppy when nurses or guests or others are around, but let him get triggered by some offhand, totally benign comment, and he'll pout and insult all through dinner. One day when Annie was visiting, she went upstairs to look at my newly-redone home office. I called after her, "Don't mind the mess on the floor!" referring to a pile of folders and papers I had yet to go through. Once she disappeared up the stairs, Dad asked me, "Did I make a mess on the floor?"

It took a moment to realize what he was talking about and I said, "Oh, no! I was talking to Annie about my office!"

And then he sneered. "Well, you were looking straight at me when you said it." Which of course I wasn't. (He's blind; how could he tell?)

This doesn't feel good, this feeling that I am being hijacked from my own life's plans in order to be available to a man who doesn't really want to be here anyway. At least that's what he says in his more morose moments. At other times, he insists that he could just move into a small apartment and maybe have someone come in once in a while and help him with his meals.

But this is from a man who takes twenty minutes to put on his watch and even then it's upside down.

Angelo wants to retire, I want to finish my second and third books, we need to downsize and sell our home and put a little money away for our golden years, but none of that can happen while my dad is living in our home. I don't *want* to resent this, but the strain limits my ability to monitor myself; when my bad behavior shows, it triggers Dad's bad behavior, and it can be a spiral that only one of us, really, can bring us out of. That would be me.

Unless properly equipped with a long-term care policy, barrels full of money or a much larger house, there just aren't many solutions in our current culture or societal construction to appropriately care for our elders. Dad and I don't typically have soul-baring, heart-to-heart conversations often, but when we do, he reveals himself to be a sad and frustrated man. He doesn't want me to give up my life to take care of him, but he has no idea how to make it any different. And even if he did, it's likely it wouldn't be an option we could consider, like assisted living, which we've already tried.

No, I'm doomed to be the worst daughter in the world until such time that one of us dies. At this point, I'm not even sure he would be the one to go first, given the above-mentioned ability to cheat death.

LOCKED-DOWN WRITER

"Not liking the look of this."
—Tweet by science journalist
HELEN BRANSWELL on January 2, 2020

It wasn't quite a month after the world changed and we all became virus vigilant that the realization hit me: being a writer and a caregiver in my own home is challenging; being a writer and a caregiver in my own home under quarantine with a high-risk parent is nearly impossible.

It is an occupational hazard that most caregivers are housebound; but as a writer, I am home anyway. When Dad first moved in with us after my mom died, it seemed like it was going to work out just fine. That's what I told myself when I was flying back and forth from Connecticut to Florida during my mom's illness and eventual death. Dad needed care, I had the room, and I worked from home. Perfect! Now, many years and a pandemic later, I am lucky to be able to get a few Facebook posts up and clear out the Instagram trolls.

What most writers need to get their work done is time. On the face of it, one would think I had *tons* of time right now to work on my book. *I* would think I had tons of time to work on my book. But a typical day in quarantine service to my dad looks like this:

- **Anywhere from 6:00 a.m. to 9:30 a.m.:** Wait in bed until I hear Dad get up to start his day.
- **One to two hours after that:** Blood sugar check, insulin shots, pills, breakfast, and chit-chat.
- **10:00-ish to 1:00-ish:** Go upstairs to my office to work (emails, planning for class, social media check-in, maybe write something . . .).
- **1:00-ish to 3:00-ish:** Lunch. Soup, sandwich, yogurt, diet soda, diet cookie—the usual.
- **3:00-ish to 4:00 p.m.:** Another escape to my office (yeah, nothing gets done at this point).
- **4:00 p.m. to 4:30 p.m.:** MiraLAX time! Back downstairs to the kitchen for MiraLAX, a diet drink, and crackers.
- **4:30-ish to 6:00 p.m.:** Back to my office to see if there's any attention span available to finish anything I started.
- **6:00-ish:** Meet Angelo on the back porch for a drink by ourselves—necessary.
- **6:30-ish to 8:30-ish:** Cocktails with dad in the kitchen and dinner.
- **9:30-ish:** Ice cream for Dad while he watches *Maddow*.
- **10:00 p.m. to 10:30-ish:** Dad's bedtime featuring night-time pills, Glucerna, eye cleanser, eye drops, and eye meds.

Every. Day.

Years ago during a pivotal trip with Angelo to his Italian birthplace, we excitedly began putting together a vision of what our lives would look like since his retirement was on the horizon. I was finally going to commit to being a full-time writer. He was looking into ways we could spend part of the year in his hometown. If I had to, I could *force* myself to write when we were in Italy.

At the time, the plan was to wrap up the promotion on my first book and begin the second—another collection of humorous essays. The plan felt nearly perfect. We had to figure out things like how to make the money we'd need to fund this perfect plan, but who was worried about that? Not us—not then.

All those plans changed when Dad moved in about six months later.

With my brother in California and my sister debilitated from fighting ovarian cancer, I was the only option. At the time, I was grateful we had the room and the resources to do it. Our hope was that he would at least hang on until Christmas because nobody thought he'd even make it till then. But he did. He survived the emotion-laden "firsts" of year one and the decline of my sister's health until she died the following year. My brother flew in several times to give Angelo and me a break, but our house—our lives—were turned over to Dad's care.

I could only devote my time and energy to one job and that job was taking care of Dad. Three meals a day, laundry, extra housekeeping, making and driving to appointments, and all the financial and medical paperwork required by one old man. And we can't forget ordering and maintaining his special supplies; as a diabetic, he needs a lot of sugar-free foods and beverages as well as all his preferred items; shirts (pocket tees), toilet paper (ultra strength), toothpaste (Crest), and mouth-wash (Listerine—not the store brand).

The years fly by when you're stressed, tired, and feeling the unpleasant seeds of resentment growing in your gut. Every time I changed the calendar hanging on the fridge—filled mostly with Dad's appointments—I counted one more year gone since my pub date. When was I ever going to be able to return to the life I had when I was whining about not having enough time but apparently had plenty? I was Dorothy in *The Wizard of Oz*: "You mean I had it all along?" And we're not even going to talk about how Angelo felt about having his part of the dream put on hold. Of course, the virus pretty much helped dash that, too.

Mostly, I beat myself up for not getting anything done in those years. Why didn't I get up earlier? Why couldn't I work after dinner? Shouldn't I have insisted that I needed some dedicated time to get my writing done? To anyone, but especially to myself? The truth is, I was so exhausted, that I could barely lift my phone to eye level to play Gummy Drop. What would I have even done with a big block of time to myself? Sleep probably. Maybe write *something*, but not an entire chapter.

Even when the pandemic subsided (loosely speaking), I still had my own lockdown in place. I'm pretty sure I'm not the only writer in the world who has cared for a parent in their home, but I bet I'm one of the few who had such a hard time with it. I always heard how *rewarded* I should feel. Actually, I was exhausted, kind of cranky, and I rarely got anything written.

However, I got this done. So there's that.

WHEN IT'S TIME TO *GO* . . .

"Everyone poops."
—Taro Gomi

I can't believe how happy I was when I thought my dad was dying this morning.

He wasn't in pain or suffering or anything—after breakfast he felt "uncomfortable" and thought he had to use the bathroom. He was in there for about fifteen minutes, and when he came out, he said he just wanted to go sit in his room. This is typical for him after breakfast; he goes into his room and watches cable news for a couple of hours while he snoozes. He might look at his phone or listen to his latest audiobook, but he always heads in there after he finishes his coffee.

This morning, after the atypical lengthy stay in the bathroom, he headed into his room but turned toward his bed instead of his padded chair. I laid out a fresh pair of pants for him because he complained that he couldn't button the ones he was wearing. I pointed them out, but he sat on them instead and turned his body to lie down on the bed. He went immediately to sleep, and I left him there to do *my* usual post-breakfast activity: go upstairs to my office and try to get something done.

But I wasn't comfortable upstairs not knowing what was going on with Dad so I came back down with my coffee and my phone to sit close by him in the living room. So I could hear him if he needed anything. But not a peep came from his room.

I got up to check several times—for the first hour he didn't move at all. His mouth was open, and he was still, but I could see his chest rise and fall with each breath. Later, he crossed his legs at the ankles and rested his hand on his forehead. And he was still breathing. I checked his breathing like I used to check my kids when they were infants; stand quietly and just watch for about a minute to determine breathing regularity. Back at my post, in my chair in the living room, I kept telling myself that "this wasn't it," this wasn't going to be the day he died. But I became aware of the feeling that I might be a little hopeful that it was.

There were so many fitting reasons for this to be his last day; the main one was that it was three years to the date that I flew home with Dad from Florida to move him in. May is a shitty month for anniversaries for our family lately. There was that first May after my mother died in January, and we decided to move Dad to Connecticut so we (I) could take better care of him. The following year on the fifteenth of May, we lost my sister to cancer (I really thought that would do him in). And then the next year, on the anniversary of her death, Dad fell leaving the house and broke his ankle. So it seemed appropriate that today would be the day he died. And it's Derby Day, perfect because we lived in Louisville, Kentucky for twenty-five years. There is no Derby this year, not in a global pandemic, but it would have been the day had they held it. It just seemed right that today would be it.

I imagined, as I have often done in the past, what it would be like to have my life back to myself. And Angelo's and my life back to ourselves. We've put aside so many things that we wanted to do as a couple that we couldn't do once we had a full-time resident needing full-time care. What I imagine is the first thing I will do on the day Dad dies—besides making all the arrangements—is nothing. I don't think I will do anything. No meals, no vigilance, no noises to wonder about, no limitations to my time, no laundry, no bathroom cleaning, no ordering supplies. Nothing. In my head, I practically float from room to room not doing anything except what I want to do. Sit here, turn on the TV, walk out to the porch, make coffee, open wine—whatever. And sleep. Sleep till whatever time I feel like getting up. Or stay in bed all day. Whatever I want to do.

As I sat glued to my chair in attendance, I also felt somewhat immobilized by the thought that today was Dad's last day. What did I say to him as he rolled his walker into his room? Was I pleasant? Or snippy, as I have become lately? I directed him to change his pants, but I wasn't insistent, was I?

At dinner the night before, I decided to talk about our three-year anniversary, but in a way that practically forced Dad to look at how much our lives had changed since his arrival and that's something he's not necessarily crazy about looking at. He remained true to form because at bedtime he snapped at me, "Thanks for telling me how wonderful everything is." Sarcastically, not really being grateful. I also felt that, had things been different—and I don't know what that would even look like—our experience could have been a much more loving and rewarding one. And I felt badly that it hadn't been.

But, right before lunch, Dad got up. Right after the last time I checked on him and he said, "I don't feel ready to go yet." (That kind of threw me—if you know what I mean.) He didn't want his usual lunch, just some yogurt and some soup. I mixed some chopped prunes into the yogurt to see if that would help him "go"—because that's what he was actually talking about. I made him some iced tea instead of the regular diet soda he usually has with his lunch to avoid another dosing of additives and chemicals, and by the end of lunch he decided he'd also like to have his postprandial diet cookie. He appeared to be feeling much better.

After lunch, Dad got back on his routine: back to his room for a news check and reading his latest book. I cleaned up the plates and utensils, swept the kitchen floor, and switched his TV to the two stations he prefers. After I took care of some things in the laundry as a result of the previous few days' minor accidents, I realized the immobilizing and stressful morning had wiped me out. I needed to take a little break. But not before Dad came back into the kitchen and headed into the bathroom. Everything on track, just as it usually is.

Until it happens for real.

THE *LAST* LAST MOVE

"Bloom where you are planted."
—Somewhat misleading quote by
THE BISHOP OF GENEVA, who
had to stay where he was.

Since my parents' "last" move from their cozy little two-bedroom home in Osprey, Florida to the well-appointed, highly-regarded retirement community of Bay Village in Sarasota, Dad has moved three more times. Technically, my mom moved one more time—into the hospice facility where she died, but that wasn't a move per se. She had only been moved there for a few days to get her strength back. It didn't come back.

Once Mom was gone, Dad couldn't stay in their one-bedroom apartment by himself, for several reasons. If my brother and I were going to continue traveling to Florida from our homes and stay with him, it just wasn't going to work for us to sleep on the pull-out couch. And, we decided, he simply couldn't be alone. Another reason was that my sister was sick and wasn't going to be taking any turns in his care, so after going through all my parents' limited belongings, we packed up what was left and moved Dad to Connecticut.

That was a big move. Honestly, I wasn't sure he'd make it through the flight from Sarasota to Atlanta to Hartford. Once home, we settled him in to our remodeled dining room-turned-bedroom, set up his pacemaker monitor, placed a few nanny cams and a baby monitor in his room, and hoped he'd be comfortable. The few belongings he had arrived a few days later, and they were stowed on one side of our garage (where they have remained). This was certainly his last move, and after a few weeks, I realized that this would be the place he died. Once that realization hit me, I became somewhat morose about the whole decision, but there was little I could do about it at that point. My home is where he lived, and at eighty-six—a diabetic, blind, traumatically brain injured, grieving widower with a heart condition—it would clearly be the place he died.

But then, there was another move. On the two-year anniversary of his move and the one-year anniversary of my sister's death, Dad decided not to wait for us to clear out the backseat of the car so we could all go to dinner with my brother-in-law and nephew and he misstepped off the front porch and shattered his ankle. After a few days in the hospital, a local skilled nursing facility became his next move. Here, shoved alongside an already established patient who took up more than half of the so-called shared room, he either sat in his bed or a wheelchair next to it while he took all his meals on a tray table and watched TV via headphones as his neighbor blared Fox News all day long. During the day he had physical therapy, and we visited him nearly every day—mostly to give him a reason to complain about all the staff and their incompetent treatment of him. I tried to ameliorate his complaints, but I have to say, most days I agreed with him. Some days, I showed up to find him in clothes that didn't belong to him. That was annoying. Then there were the days I showed up to find that he had been served two desserts. Not a great meal plan for a diabetic. (The day I showed up and his blood glucose meter registered 500 was the day I went running down to the nurses' station doing my best Shirley MacLaine impression from *Terms of Endearment*.)

When the physical therapists (not the doctors, not the nurses) decided he was ready to be discharged, he had to leave. It didn't matter that he was still non-weight-bearing and was confined to the wheelchair. When our house was evaluated for his moving back, it was clear that we were not going to come even close to being able to care for his needs; showering, toileting, eating—all of it was going to require additional modifications for him to be able to continue to recover. This decision was all on Medicare, by the way. No medical decision was involved in his discharge—when Medicare says they're done covering your stay, you're done.

Anyway. Enter a nearby assisted living facility one town over and his next move. We had been in touch with them earlier in the year as a possible respite place so Angelo and I could take some time off. The woman we had been in touch with was super helpful and eager to tell us that Dad could go there! They already had grab bars and commodes and aides and assistance. It was made for someone like my dad—in fact, one of their nurses came over to the rehab beforehand, assessed Dad for residency, and deemed him ready to go. So, instead of coming back home, he moved again—one last time—to the Villages at East Farms.

But, guess what? Go ahead—you know what I'm about to say. After about four months, we realized the assisted living facility wasn't really going to work out, and Dad moved back home. This time we put his TV in his room (a source of contention between my husband and me for almost two years before). He claimed victory when my daughter sided with him in creating a neutral zone in our living room and not having it commandeered by cable news. We took out the baby monitor but left the nanny cams. And even though we're on move number four, I still haven't gone through the boxes in the garage we brought up from Florida.

So, here we are. Again. Friends and acquaintances kept asking me the whole time he was out of the house, "Are you getting some relief from the stress?" And I'd say, "Not really, the stress is just different now." And it was true; although every day while he was somewhere else I was "off the clock" by dinner time, I was either visiting him, picking him up for appointments, or following up on medical or financial issues. Stress followed me around like a mangy puppy—I couldn't shake it and it wasn't really that cute.

Dad seemed to take all these last moves in stride, although once he was back, he was a little bit more confused; he needed a little more help to manage his insulin shots and his meds. I don't know whether there will be any more "last" moves, all I know is that when caring for an elderly parent, nothing is predictable. There just really isn't a good solution for this situation and so we go on. This could be his last move—or there could still be more in his future.

There's simply no way to know.

LAUGHING TO KEEP FROM CRYING

"When humor goes, there goes civilization."
—ERMA BOMBECK

The rumble of my dad's walker crossing into the kitchen from his room drifted up to where Angelo and I lay in our beds, stealing an afternoon nap. We weren't alarmed since Richard, visiting for the holidays, was on duty and any mishaps would be on his watch. However, on the heels of the rumbling walker came a sharp, "Dammit!" and then a muffled crash. Not a body, more like a book or perhaps a glass, hitting the floor.

"I'll get it!" my brother shouted up the stairs, followed by a succession of explosive epithets, and, oddly, sneezes.

"We're living in a group home," Angelo deadpanned to me, and we dissolved in hysterics, laughing to keep from crying, at the thought of how much our lives had changed in the last three years.

We "napped" when we needed to get away from the chaos that was now our lives. In the time that Dad had been living with us we discovered several things:

1. He isn't living with us as much as we are living with him.
2. Although I was the "child," I was sixty-one and taking care of someone else was hard! And . . .
3. We had to figure out how to maintain our privacy, sanity, and glassware while providing adequate care for an eighty-eight-year-old man. One who is, unexpectedly yet understandably, cranky.

Our lives were definitely different after he moved in; where we once grabbed a slice of toast for breakfast or lunch (or dinner), I had to plan actual meals. Balanced meals with nutrients, proteins, and colors. It was like having kids again but without a promising future. We were in charge of house-keeping, social engagements, and medical appointments. Seeing a doctor—or in his case—doctors—at his age is like painting the Golden Gate Bridge—once you paint the last stroke at the end, you have to start repainting from the begin-ning. With doctor's appointments—when you've managed to see all of them for the three-month check-ins, it's time to make another appointment with the first one again.

We tried hiring help—like the aide who ignored the detailed notes I left when she came to monitor his breakfast and help him with his insulin shots and the first thing she did was pour him a glass of sugary orange juice. We tried an assisted living facility, but after four months it was clear that Dad would be better off back with us. The biggest difference was that although they "cared" for him, they didn't love him. But we did. And so there we were once again—sweeping, driving, napping, laughing—committed to being members of our own group home.

THE END OF LIFE

"When you complain, you make yourself into a victim. When you speak out, you are in your power. So change the situation by taking action or by speaking out, if necessary or possible. Leave the situation or accept it. All else is madness."

—ECKHART TOLLE

When you take in your elderly parent to live with you to care for him (or her), it is reasonable that there is some consideration about the end of life. What will it look like? When will it be? How will I handle it? Will he have to go to a care facility, or will he die in my home? The end of life consumes my thoughts and my days. And now, after years of being a caregiver, I think about what the end of life actually looks like. Not his; mine.

After three years and who knows how many more to go, caring for my dad in my home is the end of my life as I know it. After burying my mother, we buried my sister a year later. I lost my cat. Lots of life events requiring time to mourn and process, but I had to put those feelings aside so I could attend to Dad's needs. And, when possible, my husband's, children's, and my dwindling writing career.

My days are filled with sarcasm, denial, and a perverse version of Murphy's Law. If it can be done wrong or opposite or other than any other way than it's ever been done before, he will do it. If I hand him something right side up, he will grab it wrong side down. If it's sunny outside, he'll remark on the cloudiness. If I say I'm going upstairs, he'll say he thought I had gone out. It seems he always needs the thing I just removed to wash, replace, or fix. The personal matters I have to take care of for him grow exponentially; I can't simply make one phone call to arrange an appointment, a refill, or a follow-up—there is always some other issue that must be taken care of first. The refill has expired, and this doctor doesn't take that insurance anymore, or you need a referral for that appointment.

Dad has a continuous glucose monitoring device that monitors his blood sugar. It has an app for my phone so I can always know what it is—24/7. It beeps an alarm when it dips too low, usually about three in the morning. Sometimes it's seven, prompting him to get up and start his day. Which means my day starts, too. Sometimes, he can address the alert by taking a glucose tablet I keep by his bed. But sometimes he goes looking for orange juice in the fridge, and then I have to get up to help him find a glass, put the juice back, and clean up the spill. I am on the job every minute of every day; there are no days off. No free weekends. No time to myself when I am unaware of his presence in my home. I have to be aware; he's a fall risk. Unless someone else is in the house, I can't *not* know what he's doing almost every minute.

I don't like feeling this way. I waver between knowing any day could be his last to feeling like I'll die first. How many more times will I pick up a book or read an article on caregiving that describes the immeasurable toll the job takes and how many caregivers die first, mothers, daughters, sons, and nephews? His medical complications alone point to an eventual death, but it hasn't happened yet. And every day, I grow more and more resentful and hopeless at the loss of my own life, like the dreams I imagined after my kids moved out, when my husband retired, or when I could pursue some of the interests that I've put aside all my life. The loss doesn't just affect me, but my life with my husband, and my family.

I finally succumbed to the suggestions of friends and joined a support group on social media, but it's a blessing and a curse. I'd been warned about such groups—repositories of whining and blaming and a lot of negativity—but I needed something to connect to with my growing grim feelings. So far, both men and women post daily about the trials they have endured since taking on the care of a loved one. The posts that detail a day filled with combative arguments, accidents, and rejected or thrown food are interspersed with simple posts that say something like, "My mom got her wings yesterday morning at eight. She's free of pain now." When I see those, I feel a little envious. Nobody wishes their parent to die, but that of course is the only way to be free of the 24/7 job.

The insidious knowledge that my life as I knew it has ended threads itself throughout my actions and thoughts. I get mad at him for not remembering to take off his glasses before he starts listening to his books on tape. He tends to lean forward when he's reading (and also tends to fall asleep) and the glasses fall off to the floor. Of course, he doesn't realize it or if he does, he can't see them, so eventually he'll step on them and break them. This has already happened three times, so one morning when I realized it had happened again, I became impatient. "Dad, you have to remember to take off your glasses before you start your book! This is the fourth pair in eight months!" He mumbled something about not seeing them and went back to his book. I walked out of the room feeling like a jerk.

What do I care if it's the fourth pair? He can afford to replace them, they're not that expensive. So, he drops them and steps on them. Why does it aggravate me so? One reason is probably that there are so many things to do during the day anyway that it's just one more thing I have to follow up on. When they break, I have to rig them so he can use them and order another pair. One more job that pushes my writing aside. One more responsibility I have to follow up on in case he needs a new prescription, or they don't have that style anymore, or any number of time-consuming tasks that pull me away from any kind of time I might need—even just to close my eyes for ten minutes.

I can't help but think that having these realizations, dark and hopeless as they are, are in some way helpful to my getting through this time. It magnifies for me the enormous absence of services and resources available to care for our elderly population. If we had tons of money and . . . well, just money I guess. Money doesn't buy happiness, but it does provide care, facilities, assistance, and safety.

I also know that one day I won't feel this way. I once had a woman tell me that, after more than twenty-five years of caring for her mother, when she died she wished she had done more. I kind of get that. I know my impatience is unwarranted; my resentment is within my control. I often kick myself for my short answers or insensitive remarks. When he's gone—and if I don't go first—I will miss him.

But I also think it's important to mark these feelings because it is part of the whole experience. I don't think it's particularly rewarding to be assaulted every day with negativity, displeasure, or criticism. To be the target of his misery and unhappiness. It's not fair.

For either of us.

TEN THINGS I DIDN'T SAY

*"If you don't have anything nice to say,
don't say anything at all."*
—Overused quote, possibly originated by
a bunny named Thumper.

- I told you yesterday the appointment was at 2:00 p.m.—*after* lunch—not 8:00 a.m. I don't make appointments for 8:00 a.m.
- Did you talk to Mom this way? (I might have said this one.)
- No wonder she died first. (I *didn't* say this part.)
- Do you have any idea how much work it is to take care of you?
- Dad, every time I take him to an appointment: *"Hope I didn't cause you to miss something."* No, just the last three years of my life.
- You wouldn't treat Susie like this if she were taking care of you. (She's dead. That would have been too mean.)
- Sure, we can afford a $600 walker. That's just $600 your grandchildren won't get.
- I think you already told me this story twenty times.
- Taking care of you is the worst job I've ever had.

- What was it like when you took care of your dad for three years and put off your whole life to do it? (Oh, right—you didn't.)
- How are you still alive?

My tongue had a groove in it from biting it so often. Unfortunately, it wasn't deep enough—I would sometimes let unintended remarks fly. Not that I didn't get back some real doozies in kind—some of the most hurtful things ever said to me in my life came from the mouth of my father. But mostly after he came to live with us; I don't recall his being so mean when I was growing up. Sarcastic, yes. We were all bitten by the smartass bug. But I was never the object of his scorn. Until he moved in with us.

Most days, after I woke up, I spent the fifteen minutes or so it took for me to get dressed giving myself a pep talk before heading downstairs to the kitchen. My pep talks always included the mandate: Don't be an asshole. And then I'd spend the rest of the day trying not to be one. I was not always successful. Sometimes, and this is hard to admit, a negative remark would form in my brain, I'd consider it, decide it didn't need to be said, and then I would say it anyway. If I was texting that last sentence, it would include the embarrassed face emoji next to it. I always feel bad when I've said something mean, but I couldn't always help myself from doing it.

Caring for an elderly parent in your home is difficult—even in the best of circumstances. In fact, writing essays about how hard it was were often interrupted by a mini-crisis or two. One time, it was when Dad tried to answer his phone. I heard voices coming from his room and couldn't imagine who he was talking to, so I ran downstairs to find out—Dad had answered a spam phone call and couldn't understand what the spammer was saying. Thank goodness. We kept the phone in use mostly because it was attached to his glucose monitor so he—and I—could access his blood sugar levels at a glance. And I think he liked the idea of having his own phone for the feeling of independence it gave him, even if he really couldn't always figure it out. ("You just slide your finger across the bottom, Dad.") Helpful instructions like that were rarely appreciated and usually elicited an "I *know*" in response.

For a while, we tried having him see a therapist to help him deal with his limitations and hopefully give him a more positive outlook. Every once in a while, I joined him. A kind of weird couples counseling. One time, he told her that I called him "skanky" and *that's* why he was so disagreeable. I was immediately defensive—of course, I never called him that! I barely like using that word to begin with, and I'd never use it to refer to my father! I couldn't even imagine where he got that until I realized he meant "snarky." Now, that I did accuse him of. Because he was. But he continued telling others—strangers, even—that I called him skanky. No matter how many times I tried explaining that I never used that word to describe him, he was never able to let it go.

Every day then was simply a race to bedtime without actually saying or doing something I would regret. I didn't *have* to point out that his shirt was buttoned wrong, or his shoes were on the wrong feet. I didn't *have* to moan and groan when I pulled his laundry basket out of his room or dragged the vacuum in. I didn't have to remind him, "I've already told you that," or "You told me that yesterday." If I could get to the end of the day with maybe a 75 percent success rate, I felt like I deserved the glass of wine I couldn't wait to pour myself.

It wasn't easy. I'm both glad we could care for him and simultaneously exhausted that we still had to. He survived so much. It wasn't his plan to land in my dining room at the end of his life, and he was even worse than I am about managing his snarky and sarcastic comments.

Oh, wait—that's where I got it from.

PLAYING GOD

"Life is God's novel. Let him write it."
—Isaac Bashevis Singer

It feels like everyone is dying these days except my dad. And if you think that sounds cruel and heartless, trust me, you're right. It is. I hate that I feel that way.

Midcareer actors, young athletes, and children with cancer. People for whom it's not fair, it's not their time. They had so much to live for. Why them? And then, the unspoken next sentence: And why not Dad?

It is the utmost level of unfairness to me that children die when dementia patients continue to live. I grieve when I hear another case of cancer cutting short the life of a vibrant, active adult when a man who can't put his shoes on the right feet lives on and on and on. Wives losing beloved husbands, babies without their mothers, fathers grieving their sons. And in households and nursing homes all over the country, millions of dementia patients live out their days, totally incapacitated and not only unable to communicate their distress but unable to seek release from it.

This is probably the most uncomfortable of feelings that comes up for me as a caregiver. I do not like feeling that it's unfair that Dad lives while others die. Do I think he is less deserving? I don't think so, but he just seems so unhappy. I know for certain that is not what I want for myself—or for my children. I've already forbidden all three of them to take me in to live with them. Why do people live past their ability to experience joy? God kind of fucked up in that department. He should've timed the expiration date on the ability to experience joy to coincide right at the time of passing.

But it's really not my decision, is it? And actually, there are times that I think he is still able to feel joy and experience life. I think the capacity is within him, but it's not always accessible. He doesn't contribute to the day-to-day responsibilities of running a home, having a job, and living a social life, but he loves it when his children and grandchildren come to visit. He is raring to go when we plan a visit with family or friends in his hometown and don't count him out when it's time to eat! Although he maintains that he "doesn't eat very much," he is the first one to put away a cinnamon scone or a dish of chocolate ice cream or a (small) plate of fettuccine Alfredo.

It's no one's decision when to die, not even your loved one's. How many times did I walk by the woman sitting quietly in her wheelchair in the lobby of the skilled nursing facility in the building where my parents lived in Florida and wonder what her story was? Their residence building included the facility as a "benefit" to the residents, euphemistically referred to as "the second floor." Because my parents' apartment was one floor above, I typically took the stairs down to visit whichever of my parents was being treated there at the time. At the end of my mom's life they were both there for a short time together. The stairway opened right into the reception area of the floor and this woman—whose name I never learned, or even inquired about—was parked there every day—just to the right of the upholstered visitor's chairs and next to the tall potted palm as if she were being camouflaged. She wore a housedress—not really "dressed" but not in pj's either and she listed a little to the left in her chair. Sometimes she seemed to be humming softly to herself, other times she was quiet. In my comparative youthfulness, I always smiled at her when I strode by on my way elsewhere, but I don't think she ever noticed. At least she didn't acknowledge me. She may be the first person that made me think, "Why is she still here? What kind of life is she living?"

And the answer, of course, is it's nobody's business. It's not even a valid question, is it? If any of us could even answer the question, "How much longer do we have?" would we even want the answer? As many times as I've felt frustrated at the rate of deaths among the seemingly healthy and more deserving of life, I have experienced a similar number of times when I want to be sure Dad is feeling loved and cared for. Yes, he's a burden, but he's my burden.

What I have to keep in mind is that the way I feel now is not going to be the way I feel when he's gone. I will miss him. I will wish we had more time. I will love him. Right now, when I wake up every morning, I wonder if he will, too. And I don't feel sad that he might not. I crave the freedom of my life and the freedom I didn't even know I had before. And, ironically, knowing that I will miss Dad and have an outpouring of grief when he's gone doesn't help temper the frustration I feel at having to continue to care for him in his increasing and demeaning needs.

God help me.

HUSBANDS

"My mother buried three husbands—
and two of them were only napping."
—Rita Rudner

One of life's little ironies: My husband was angry because I wasn't taking care of him, and my dad was angry because I *was* taking care of him!

Not that Angelo would admit to it, of course. He thought—and I know this because he often told me—that he understood that I couldn't be available to him at the time. He "got" it. Which was also ironic—because as far as I was concerned, he continued to be at the top of my priority list, albeit with less time and energy. And this made *me* angry. How could I expend so much time and attention on the two old men living in my house and neither one of them appreciated it?

Ready for another irony? Angelo had every right to feel the way he did. Even though I didn't like it so much, I felt like he should have the room to say and do some of the things he did because he was pretty much bearing the financial brunt of our caregiving adventure. Although he had been eyeing retirement pretty closely, he ended up supporting a household of adults, none of whom were contributing very much to the care and upkeep. Me, because I was too busy with the responsibilities of taking care of Dad, and Dad wasn't because he was incapable of anything really significant. He contributed what he could financially, but it wasn't like we put an in-law addition on to the house. And that makes him unhappy, too. Dad was always a doer, a problem solver. Knowing he can't even so much as carry in a bag of groceries is a constant reminder of what a burden he is.

One Sunday morning, I was getting ready to leave the house for a rare two-hour outing to attend a friend's baby shower. As I was drying my hair—also a rare occurrence—I heard a faint noise from downstairs. It sounded angry—like shouting. But that couldn't be, right? I stopped the blow-dryer and listened more closely—yep! Shouting! I ran downstairs to the living room to find Angelo standing over Dad, who was seated in his chair, and both of them practically snarling at each other. I got between them and tried walking Angelo back into the kitchen as Dad sputtered insults at Angelo. Angelo was seething—a state I think I've seen maybe once or twice in our lives. Once in the kitchen, Angelo appeared to settle down a bit—but not much.

In the living room, still seated in his blue chair, Dad gripped the TV remote—apparently the cause of the blowup. From what I understood, all Angelo did was lower the volume on the TV. Dad often dozed while watching the news and would keep the remote clutched in his hand, which could result in his accidentally raising the volume to blast because of the vice-grip he has on the volume button. It happened all the time. But this time, when Angelo went in to lower it, Dad woke up and got defensive about his mistake. Angelo scolded Dad for not realizing what he was doing, and Dad insulted Angelo about how he thought he knew everything. It was awful. I debated not going to the shower, but in fact, the only thing I wanted to do was run out of the house and never come back.

About twenty minutes later, Angelo came into the living room and apologized to Dad. Dad was not exactly receptive to it, but he eventually accepted the apology. Angelo was sincere and thoughtful in his apology, and I believed him. Because, to this day, I also know he doesn't like acting like that himself. No one does, really. Angelo didn't like that his anger got triggered, Dad didn't like being reminded that he's an incompetent old man, and I didn't like the level of anger and frustration in my home when the whole purpose for this damn arrangement was to provide a loving and caring environment.

Ironic, isn't it?

THE MiraLAX SPOON

---

*"The difference between a strong man and a weak one
is that the former does not give up after a defeat."*
—WOODROW WILSON

W ho knew a spoon could be an object of contention? Especially when used for MiraLAX, the popular laxative that
actually has the word "gentle" in its description?

Years ago, Dad was "prescribed" the laxative to combat
some possible side effects of a medication he was taking. Of
course, he stopped the medication, but he hung on to his
MiraLAX habit. Every afternoon at promptly 4:00 p.m., Dad
would go to the kitchen, fill the dispenser cap with the silvery
magic powder, *tap–tap–tap* it into his glass of diet drink, stir it
up, and pair it with several squares of dark chocolate. (I think
the habit stuck because of the chocolate.) Many things in
his life have changed over the years, due to an assortment of
reasons, but the one constant in his life was MiraLAX time.

Until he came to live with us.

Even though I knew the importance of keeping as much
consistency as possible, I made changes to some of his routines as
we combined households. At some point, I transferred the stash of

MiraLAX into a large plastic deli container. It was easier to open and the red, double-ended measuring spoon he used fit easily inside. One end of the spoon was the "correct" measurement and the other end was a little bigger. I often worried that he would use the "wrong" end, and sometimes he did. But Angelo and I figured, how much harm could it be? And it still allowed him to maintain one of his rituals within his limited capabilities. Not that *he* thought he had limited capabilities. Besides, I was usually within eye or earshot and could step in if a mistake was made.

Then, the broken ankle and resulting three-month stay in a skilled nursing facility took the ritual out of his hands. His meds and the MiraLAX were delivered by the nurses, but not at four, and not accompanied by chocolate. Or anything else. When he eventually transitioned to the assisted living residence to continue with his recovery, the habit was back in his control. Except, since I wouldn't be there to monitor him every day, I switched out the spoon. It was still red and plastic, but it had only one end—the correct measurement one. He could forget to take it, but he wouldn't end up dumping an extra dose of the laxative into his juice.

About three months later, after the assisted living place didn't work out, Dad and his MiraLAX came home again. After all the transitions and changes, Dad's ability to concentrate had suffered. It wasn't so much that he made mistakes—I knew I couldn't keep *all* of them from happening. Like spilling juice—the probability of which corresponded to the color of the drink. The darker the flavor, the more likely it was to get dumped on the kitchen floor. But one day, he tried mixing the dose with pure lime juice. So, I began pouring the juice but let him tap in the MiraLAX and stir it a thousand times to make sure it was mixed in. He was a chemist—that's how you do it.

And then I changed the spoon—again.

I traded out the red plastic spoon with a metal one because I noticed when the plastic one was dipped into the container, static electricity sprayed minuscule grains of MiraLAX across the counter. I didn't want that stuff making its way into my dinner prep so when he or I added the laxative, it didn't end up all over the place. It was my way of allowing him some independence and keeping my kitchen tidier all at the same time.

One day, when I lined up the MiraLAX container, the pre-filled cup with diet lemonade, and a small plate of Wheat Thins (he made that change after the assisted living experience), he stopped as he pulled out the spoon. "Where's my other spoon?" he demanded in kind of an insistent tone.

"Oh, we stopped using that a few months ago," I told him.

"I just used it last week. I don't remember this one," he continued.

"We've been using that one for a while, Dad. Maybe you don't remember that we switched."

He looked at me suspiciously and carried on with his MiraLAX ministrations. I really didn't think it was that big of a deal. And I didn't pay that much attention to his complaint until it came up again.

Because you know it did.

Suddenly, every other day, it was a similar observation: "Where is my usual spoon?" or "This isn't the right measurement!" or "Get me my regular spoon!" (*Regular* spoon. It was hard not to make a joke about that one.) And I held to the fact that the new metal one was one we had been using for months, and it seemed to work just fine.

But then, without going into too much detail, Dad had what we'll just call a "bathroom incident." It was sudden, embarrassing, and required lots and lots of cleanup. Including a shower. For both of us.

Again, the spoon was back in the spotlight.

"I think that spoon is the wrong dose," he said a day or so after the incident. "That must have been what the problem was. It's the wrong spoon."

"It's the same dose you've taken for the last five years. It wasn't the MiraLAX. It must have been something you ate." I was trying to reassure him, but instead, I made things worse.

"The spoon I use has two sides. I must have used the wrong side," he went on.

"That spoon doesn't exist anymore. I tossed it out last summer when you went to the Village." (Whoops, maybe I shouldn't have said that.)

"You *tossed* it out?" This was posed as a bit of an accusation, as if I had sold the family silver to a peddler.

More sidelong glances followed, and a kind of a *harrumph* of begrudging concession as he nibbled his crackers and sipped his juice.

Until the next time.

"We should probably get that other spoon back . . ."

The truth is, he often didn't remember any of those conversations. The only thing he did remember was that he used to do more stuff on his own and then he did less, with more people doing it for him. Bits and pieces of his former abilities danced in and out of his recollection when he attempted a task he'd done with ease and skill most of his life. He'd probably forgotten more than he remembered, so hanging on to whatever he could do was all he had left.

So, every day around four, when I heard the rumble of his walker enter the kitchen and head toward the cabinet where the supplies were kept, I'd head down to join him and provide as little or as much help as he needed. Whether he remembered or not.

The MiraLAX ritual endured till the end.

CAREGIVING AND A PANDEMIC DON'T MIX (SO DON'T EVEN TRY)

"Oil and water don't mix."
—Proverb

In most ways, I am very well suited to a global pandemic. I am a supreme homebody. I love snow days for their built-in "can't go anywhere now!" mechanism. With the pandemic, I'm holed up in my house—which I love—and I can't go *anywhere*. Bonus! Not to the store, not to my kids' houses, not to my friends, not to the office. No meetings, no appointments, no errands, no forgotten errands. No exercise class!

As a caregiver, though, the scenario changes a little bit. Once the world shut down and we all became quarantined in our homes, another layer of stress became evident very quickly. What little work I had, I'm doing from home. Angelo is also able to do his work—as a therapist—from home. The supervised visitation program we ran has been suspended; we had to lay off the one woman we had working for us. The only person we have coming in is the visiting nurse who has to change the wound from Dad's broken ankle two times a week. It used to be three different nurses three times a week, but I asked the agency to limit the number of people who were coming in and out of the house and the one who still comes doesn't work on weekends. I am the new weekend wound nurse.

For his part, Dad doesn't really understand what's going on—really. He can watch the news, talk about current events, and mansplain everything that I need to do to deal with the virus, but he also forgets how many insulin shots he's done, can't follow a conversation at times, and takes too many glucose tablets when he gets paranoid about his blood sugar level—which is constantly monitored 24/7.

His paranoia is also having an impact on his understanding of our living situation. He asks why Christopher didn't come into the house when he dropped by to check on us or when is Annie coming to dinner with her family. When I remind him about physical distancing due to the virus, he acts suspicious of my response. He responds to anything Angelo says or does as though he is some sort of interloper in the house and treats him with furtive glances and sarcastic remarks. When I go to the kitchen porch to pick up a package from outside, he offers to bring it in for me, but I tell him I have to leave it in the living room for a day first, to supposedly decontaminate it, which he doesn't understand and isn't even able to go pick up the package anyway. And then he gets mad.

I am in the house day in and day out; we three are all in the high-risk category, but my dad is clearly the highest risk. I'm not going out at all if I don't have to. And I know it's still a risk for Angelo to run out to the store, but we have little else we can do. We're limiting visitors, deliveries—all manner of contact we can control. As a diabetic, Dad needs—or is at least used to need—a specific menu for his meals. I never realized what a luxury it was to run out to the store for diet soda or no-sugar yogurt when we ran low. Another complication is that Dad is declining even more—when he saw Angelo and me cleaning out the pantry (to make room to store bulk items), Dad thought we were sealing up the windows and doors to keep the virus out—as if it were airborne.

Taking care of ourselves has reached a new level of both importance and imagination. Even though it feels bad, keeping some distance from Dad is imperative. He was once the man who raised me and encouraged me. Now he's the man who insists that my husband is only being nice to him for the recognition. (From whom, I often wonder.) Hours of self-care time have evolved into minutes of self-care. Now, I take fifteen minutes after I clean up from lunch and sit outside and play a game on my phone. When we used to call my dad to the table for "cocktail time" when we started dinner, Angelo and I now have our own private cocktail time for ten minutes outside on the back patio. When we come back inside, we let Dad know we're ready for cocktails and prepare his snacks and wine spritzer.

We are lucky to have a comfortable home and the means to get food into the house and keep the lights on. But being tethered this tightly to my responsibility had ignited a resentment in me that I am having trouble managing. I can't get to half the things I had enjoyed before Dad moved in and needed constant care, like picking up my grandson from school or having a sleepover with my daughter one night a week. Add a pandemic to those limitations and my outside (as it were) activities have evaporated to zero. I can manage a couple of writing classes if they're online, but write another book? Ha. If I were quarantined alone with Angelo, who knows what it would look like. But with my dad, it's not like being a homebody at all. It's more like serving a sentence.

In my office upstairs, there are no fewer than four scented candles burning that I started burning while I write. I got the idea from a friend who lights a "writing candle" when she begins her work, and I appropriated it as a way to formalize my writing time. I also think the aroma helps to transport me psychologically since I'm not going anywhere physically. It's hard to see an end in sight—especially when there are so many possible endings. Will the virus go away? Will we get vaccines? Will one of us get sick? Will one of us need hospitalization? Will one of us die?

Caring for my dad was already a full-time job. Anyone who says differently is selling something. (Perhaps scented candles.) Caring for someone who doesn't think he needs to be cared for is an exercise in frustration, and trying to keep him safe during a pandemic is nearly impossible. We've been reinventing our lives on a constant basis since Dad moved in.

I guess we just keep going.

SIX WORD MEMOIRS—CAREGIVER VERSION

"Brevity is the soul of wit."
—Shakespeare

"He can't be alone!" Me, neither.

Once my dad, now my job.

The past becomes the future's dream.

Planning only gets results in theory.

Whose bright idea was this anyway?

He's still a "we", missing Mom.

"Where is my...?" It's right here.

Having "me time" requires another me.

This was a fun day! Poof!

He's here, sometimes I see him.

You don't know jack about shit.

I remember you! I remember you.

Memory Lane is our favorite street.

Consumed with living, consumed with dying.

Fiercely independent, hopelessly helpless, desperately trying.

Vigilance is 24/7, rest is not.

The end comes faster than expected.

There is no guilt in caregiving.

LET ME KNOW WHAT I CAN DO

*"If you're not doing what
someone needs, it isn't help."*
—ME

I can't recall if it was someone famous who said this or if it was a friend of mine, but I've remembered it since I heard it. This person had just suffered a loss, and a friend said to them the oft-repeated phrase, "Let me know if there's anything I can do."

This is a well-meaning, yet often benign, offer heard over and over by those grieving and suffering. This person suggested that it bordered on offensive to say this as it gave the grief-stricken yet one more thing to do: find something for their friend to help them with.

I've kept it with me ever since I heard it because I am one of those people who say it: *Let me know if there's anything I can do.* I felt bad that those words might be heard as offensive, so from that point going forward, I tried to ameliorate it by adding the disclaimer: If something comes up that you wish someone could do for you, please don't hesitate to let me know. But every time the words came out of my mouth, I immediately wanted to take them back, even though every time I genuinely wanted to help by taking something off the grieving person's plate. Now that I think about it, no one has ever asked for my help. So, what does one say—or better yet, do?

The answer can't be nothing, can it? Over the last few years, as we lost my mom, had my dad move in, lost my sister, and had my dad in the nursing facility, there were plenty of times I wished someone would come and do something for me. I had been grieving at some level for years, so of course I needed help! I was a mess! But I was also the oldest child *and* a caregiver, so it wasn't easy for me to accept—or even conceive of—help from another. And I had offers; there are good people in my life and my struggles don't get past them, but it is difficult to know what to do or say. Especially when the situation is chronic: How many times can you offer condolences or comfort before you get tired of hearing it yourself?

For example, so many people offered to bring me a meal, but I never knew how to accept that. With Dad being diabetic, I plan our meals pretty carefully—what if someone wanted to drop off a pizza? Which would have been wonderful, but I would still have to supplement it with veggies or a salad. Then there was the possibility of the popular family-style meal—an enormous dish of pasta or other casserole that requires divvying up and figuring out how to store it. As tempting as it was to have a meal delivered to me so all I'd have to do was sit down with a fork and knife in my hand and open my mouth, it mostly felt like more work for me.

There were often offers from people letting me know they could run an errand. But unless I was organized enough to keep a running shopping list at close hand (I'm not), I didn't really know what I needed when those offers arrived. Honestly, it was easier to place an order online and have it delivered to my door. (Now, a gift card for online orders? There's a great idea—for someone. Hint, hint.)

I like to believe the "let me know what I can do" offer is sincerely given. It's just that during a time of crisis or sadness, the last thing anyone thinks about is how to organize their needs. I understand what that person meant by adding another burden, but I have decided not to see it that way. I appreciate each and every friend who offered his or her time and energy to help me. I truly believe they mean it from the bottom of their hearts. As a way to help the helpers, I've come up with a few suggestions.

DON'Ts:

- Don't leave anything on the porch that will spoil, melt, or attract neighborhood pets or wild animals.
- It's okay to drop in but don't stay. On second thought, don't drop in, either. It might have been a really draining day.
- Don't worry that your offer is offensive—and don't get insulted if it's not accepted. It may just be that your friend doesn't know what she needs. So . . .
- Don't abandon her. She needs you, just in different ways for a while.

DOs:

- Do check in. A text, an email, a voicemail. A check-in is almost guaranteed to bring a smile to someone's face.
- Do drop off a treat. A couple of magazines, a good book you just finished, a scented candle, or fancy hand cream. Chocolates are okay, too, but just make sure you note the first "don't" above. A handpicked bouquet of wildflowers in a mason jar sitting on the front porch does wonders for the mood. (Don't leave anything that has to be unpacked, trimmed, or requires a vase being found. *Nuh-uh.* Don't do it.)
- On the other hand, company can be nice, as long as the visit is short and sweet. Fifteen minutes—max. Treats are

welcome for the short visit, too, you know, like a special coffee creamer, or a bottle of wine.

- Do call and say, "I'm at the store. Do you need coffee?" or "I'm picking up food. How's an order of fries sound?" If they don't answer, don't worry about it.

The offer of solace is a human connection. Maybe instead of saying, "Let me know if there's anything I can do," we can transition to, "I don't know what to do right now, but I love you and I'm here."

SORRY ABOUT THE PANDEMIC

*"If there is a worse time for something
to go wrong, it will happen then."*
—MURPHY'S COROLLARY

It wasn't quite a month after the whole world changed and we became permanent inmates of our own homes that I realized the whole pandemic was my fault. I happened upon a tweet from some guy on Twitter who asked, "Be honest: What did you do to cause the pandemic?" That guy had decided to start saving money and go to movie theaters more. I responded, "I finally hired some in-home aides to help take care of my dad so I could get out of the house a couple days a week and have some time to myself, maybe even get a little writing done. I'm pretty sure that's what did it."

Once Dad returned home at the end of November 2019 from the assisted living facility that hadn't worked out very well, I knew I had to make plans so I could still get out of the house a couple of times a week. At the time, I only taught one class, had some office hours with students, and continued to help out in the supervised visitation practice Angelo and I ran.

So far, I could get most of that done with Angelo or family and friends covering.

Soon after Christmas, however, the anger and resentment that darkened Dad's daily mood, and which had started almost as soon as he moved back in with us, manifested in his lashing out at Angelo (mostly) and me when he felt frustrated in his inability to accomplish daily tasks. We realized that if we didn't find some professional help, the strain of returning to full-time caregiving was going to do me in. The only regular help we'd previously had was my brother-in-law Stephan coming for a couple hours on Mondays and Brigitte, a young woman who worked in our practice, who came for a few hours on Fridays. Dad was okay with both of them because he could act like it was just Stephan coming by for a visit and Brigitte was his friend, just stopping by to chat.

However, in late January, it was clear we needed to make finding an agency or at least a professional aide a priority. The stress was getting to me, and even though I knew all the conventional wisdom of taking care of oneself when caring for another, conventional wisdom doesn't always tell you how to make it happen. You know what I mean—"stay in touch with family and friends!" But how do you do that when you can't leave the house for more than an hour? I did my best to stay connected to the things that made me feel like I was still in charge of my life, but sometimes the strain of doing even that was too much to bear.

In February, after several attempts at getting outside help (too unreliable, too expensive, too complicated, too unwelcome), we found an agency that met our requirements. Whether or not I had a class to teach, a writers' group meeting to go to, or needed a couple of hours to myself, we were going to be able to schedule enough hours during the week to cover it all. It took three aides before we found the right one, and she began the first week of March. She was great! But, by Friday of the second week, she called out sick due to a sore throat and with the growing threat of the coronavirus, I canceled the rest of her services.

Once the virus hit the United States, the high-risk populations were identified and it basically included all three of us: me, Angelo, and Dad. I decided on shuttering the doors and staying inside. Actually, it took me a couple of weeks to seal us all up—I taught a class, I went to a meeting, I took Dad to two of his appointments. But after that—done. No more going out, no one coming in. Not even my children. And no more aides.

So, it was my fault. I'm sorry.

MEMORY LANE

"My memory is so bad.
How bad is it?
How bad is what?"
—Somewhat funny joke
about memory

Nothing says, "we don't really remember things the same" than having your elderly parent living at home with you.

First of all, memories as you know them will be challenged. It's almost like all the combined memories of everyone in the family get tossed into a giant memory Spin Art machine and they all get spattered about, blending into each other like so many reds, yellows and blues. Places exchange places, people become older, younger. Dates and important events interchange as easily as slipping a blood pressure pill into a spoonful of applesauce.

For example, in an effort to evoke kinder, simpler times rather than have another frustrating conversation about why he can't stay up until midnight and watch Carson (because it's not Carson anymore), you might say, "Remember when the family drove to Florida to visit Grandma and Papa in our old green Rambler station wagon? It was so hot, we had to keep the windows open even if it rained!" However, be prepared for a response something like, "We didn't keep the windows open!

We had air-conditioning, because it was the Mercury, not the Rambler. And we were visiting Nana!"

Like that.

Another issue that comes up with memory is that the caregiver is often confused with--or wishfully thought of as--the missing spouse. I don't know how many times Dad has said to me, "Wasn't that when *we* moved to Louisville?" when talking about putting the new patio in *our* backyard. Or, "Remember when *we* tried mussels? *We* just didn't like them." However, being referred to as a different person is fluid and can change several times during one conversation.

One day Dad and I had a long, *long*, conversation about medical procedures. I started correcting him about dates and places, but he began to get testy. Actually, I'm sure it was mostly frustration, but his frustration comes out as testiness. And sometimes sarcasm. And then accusations. "How would you remember anyway? You weren't there!"

Nearly every article I read on caring for an elderly parent with memory issues (including, but not limited to, Alzheimer's, dementia, plain old aging, etc.) suggests going along with the delusion so as not to distress the elder. I get this to a certain point. Nobody wants to have an argument about whether or not there's a little girl standing behind the chair in the living room. (There wasn't.) And what's to gain from correcting that belief? Nothing. That conversation goes something like this:

Dad: Do you see her?
Me: No. Who?
Dad: That little girl. Behind the chair.
Me: I don't see her . . . what does she look like?
Dad: What do you mean you don't see her? She's right there!

And so on . . .

This was clearly a no-win situation—Dad couldn't convince me there was a little girl and I literally couldn't see her. (Because she wasn't there, remember?) In hardly any of the articles I read did it mention what slipping down the rabbit hole does to the caregiver. In my case, I was already living in an alternate reality—caring for a man who I used to totally and completely look up to. A man who, when I walked in well past curfew in high school with the lame excuse that I was late coming home from the basketball game because a dog ran out in front of the car and we had to stop the car, go look for the dog, find its owner and then return the poor little scared pup, would angle his head, look me straight in the eye, and without even uttering a word, sent me the clear message I was busted. I was raised in a family that held truth to be of utmost importance in becoming a "good person." Dad was the exemplar, we all tried to live up to his own commitment to this model that he demonstrated every day.

So, was I going to try and join this same man in a delusion that was simply that? A delusion? No, I was not. It felt like I was being asked to go against everything I was taught—everything he had taught me. This didn't mean I didn't do everything in my power to join him in his reality, which I believed to be a very different thing. His reality was that he was a man with a once powerful brain being attacked by the vagaries of age. The memory loss, memory jumble or even flat-out fantasy could show up at any time, any day, and it's not easy to be ready for them. But then there were the moments when he was there as he always was. Even if he showed up for a minute, with his sharp wit and accurate facts, I wasn't going to disrespect that man by pretending I was Mom or that we suddenly had a new dog.

Not after all I remember about being his daughter.

AFTER

OTHER VALUABLE CONSIDERATION

ATTORNEYS AT LAW

PLEASE
REPLY TO:

August 10, 2022

E-FILED VIA TURBOCOURT &
SENT VIA CERTIFIED MAIL

Region #22 Probate District (PD-22)

Re: Estate of Warren Oscar Eastman

Dear Judge-

Please find enclosed the original Last Will and Testament, dated March 26, 1998 for the Estate of Warren Oscar Eastman.

Today, we have e-filed a copy of the Will, along with the Affidavit for Filing Will not Submitted for Probate (PC-211), Affidavit in Lieu of Probate of Will/Administration (PC-212), Appearance of Attorney (PC-183), death certificate, and paid funeral bill.

Please note that the Affidavit in Lieu of Administration includes a claim by the decedent's daughter, Cynthia Eastman, in the amount of $6,200. This claim is being filed to fulfill the decedent's intentions of giving his daughter his vehicle. Mr. Eastman had signed the back of his registration naming Cynthia as the beneficiary. Unfortunately, the new registration came at the beginning of the COVID pandemic and the step of signing the beneficiary designation before a witness was overlooked. Further, prior to the decedent's death, my office was preparing to file a Medicaid application and transfer all of the decedent's assets, including those owned by his revocable trust, to Cynthia Eastman using the Other Valuable Consideration exception to Medicaid's general rule of gifts resulting in a penalty period. As you know, to qualify for Other Valuable Consideration, the decedent had to live with and receive care from Cynthia Eastman sufficient to keep him out of a nursing home for two or more years. In May of 2019, when we first met with the decedent, he was legally blind, had diabetes and mild cognitive impairment, and required the use of a walker or cane due to balance problems. The above health issues meant that he needed a fair amount of assistance and supervision.

Cynthia had already stopped working for approximately two years in order to provide her father with the care and assistance he needed. Below are details regarding the assistance provided in the summer of 2019; the care only increased until the date of Mr. Eastman's death:

A. Bathing: supervision and assistance with getting in and out of the shower due to balance issues;

B. Dressing: Laying out his clothing due to vision issues and because he would occasionally forget where things were located. Occasionally, he would require hands on assistance with putting his pants on because he would try to put them on upside down or put both feet in the same leg hole;

C. Feeding and Meal Preparation: Prepare meals and cut food due to vision problems. Reminders to eat diabetes appropriate foods and portions. Clean up after spills due to poor vision;

D. Medication Administration: Reminders to check insulin levels. Filled weekly pill box (5 to 6 medications taken 3 to 4 times daily) and made sure all prescriptions were refilled. Change Dexcom (constant glucose monitor) weekly. Review insulin dosage before administered to make sure it was accurate.

E. Ambulating: Supervision. He was legally blind and unsteady on his feet.

If you have any question regarding this matter, do not hesitate to contact our office.

Very truly yours,

cc: Mrs. Cynthia L. Eastman (w/ Will and e-filed documents)

THE DAY HE DIED

"We're all just walking each other home."
—RAM DASS

It wasn't on a Sunday afternoon, like Mom, or on the fifteenth of the month, like Mom and Susie. It wasn't on a Tuesday, or during an evening of wild weather—high winds, storminess, and tornado watches—like Susie. It was a Wednesday, the seventeenth of February at his regular bedtime—around ten. Right after *Rachel Maddow*. I had my hand on his heart as it stopped, and I cried as if I had never expected it to happen at all.

Richard had arrived in Connecticut the day before. He stayed up most of that night with Dad as he was restless: trying to get up, needing to be cleaned, and having his Depends changed. I went down once or twice to help, but otherwise, I tried staying in bed and getting some sleep. I was scheduled to get my second COVID-19 vaccination the next afternoon, and I had been hearing about all the terrible side effects of it: fever, chills, aches. I was glad Richard was there so I wouldn't have to worry about having to take care of Dad if I were incapacitated.

About two weeks earlier on February 1—it was a Monday—Dad got up, ate breakfast, and went back to bed, complaining of nausea and fatigue. That definitely wasn't like him, but that was how the next several days went; Dad slept through meals, was up and restless at night, occasionally skipped insulin and pills and was basically what Angelo and I referred to as "off." There were times he couldn't even bear his own weight, appearing as though he thought he was walking but not moving his feet. One of those times was when he "really had to go to the bathroom," and we ended up making a makeshift bedpan on his bed so he could "go." I wasn't sure I was going to be able to keep up that kind of care, but we were actually in the middle of arranging to hire a caregiver that week. When his behavior took a turn, we postponed it for the time being to figure out what was going on with Dad and to determine whether or not we'd need a different kind of care going forward.

By Friday morning that first week, I finally called two of Dad's doctors. I called the endocrinologist because I had some questions about his unusual blood sugar readings—they were atypically high, especially for not eating much or taking insulin. The doctor wasn't in, but her nurse recommended I call Dad's primary care doctor—or take him to the emergency room. When I called the primary doc, his nurse recommended I call Dad's endocrinologist and also recommended the emergency room if I had concerns. I did have concerns, mainly about taking him to the ER. There was no way I was going to drop him off at a hospital mid-pandemic and not be allowed to stay with him or visit him if he had to be admitted. No. Way.

So we kept him home and that evening, he seemed to be coming back to his old self. He had a long conversation with Richard just before dinner and appeared to have his old appetite back. He even had dessert while he checked in with his favorite cable news friend—Rachel Maddow. Bedtime was normal-ish. I gave him half a dose of melatonin to see if it would help him stay asleep so he wouldn't have to get up to use the bathroom several times that night. And it worked! It was the first night in a long time that he slept through the night.

Meanwhile, Angelo stayed in contact with the homecare registry owner. When he described what we had been dealing with, she practically insisted that we contact our local hospice agency, and that they'd come out and do an assessment. Angelo and I just looked at each other: Hospice? We knew what hospice meant—less than six months to live. Was that what was happening? We had a virtual intake the next day—Sunday— where a social worker reviewed our situation and took notes on Dad's condition. She said she'd send out a nurse the following morning for an in-person evaluation. After Friday's rally, Dad went back to mostly sleeping and needing lots of help with the things he was mostly able to do on his own: brushing his teeth, going to the bathroom, changing his clothes, and eating.

Monday morning changed everything—again. The hospice nurse admitted him, and a flurry of phone calls was now required to put all the new services in place. I asked Angelo to be in charge of that. I was wiped out from the increased physical caring for Dad and the emotional rollercoaster of what it all meant. A hospital bed was brought in, along with a transport wheelchair, and a commode for his room. Hospice delivered all the supplies: Depends, mattress pads, and even his medications were transferred over to hospice. Well, most of them; some had to be maintained the regular way, including the insulin—which he wasn't taking anyway. I grew frustrated at how much more paperwork and how many phone calls I had to oversee when all I wanted to do was to make sure Dad was okay—which he wasn't.

Dad grew more and more "off." He slept most of the days, but at night he was up—restless and needing to use the bath-room. I took his walker away so he wouldn't try walking to the bathroom—a mere ten steps away from his bedroom—but, as I discovered via the "Dad Cam" we had in his room, he found the commode and tried using that as a walker. I was up more times that week than at any other time since he had moved in. Some nights I slept in the living room so I could both hear him if he got up and get to him sooner if he tried managing the bathroom trips solo. He was getting weak and frustrated and not all that happy about my forcing him to "just pee in the Depends."

We celebrated my birthday that week—and I use the term "celebrated" loosely. Not that Angelo and my kids didn't do their best to make it a special day—they did. But with the stress of not knowing what was going on with Dad, the whole evening kind of crashed and burned with everyone retreating to their rooms. But on Friday, Dad rallied again—it made me wonder if he was one of those TGIF folks when he worked. Another Friday night and it seemed that he was back—slightly cranky and frustrated but engaged and smart. Always smart. During pre-dinner cocktails that night, we called Richard to ask him a question about poetry. Richard's regular calls that week had been interrupted by Dad's "off" behavior, so we chatted with him about the poet Wendell Berry and the movie *A Man for All Seasons* while we had our snacks and wine.

But, then, the next morning, there was another downturn. I made Dad French toast for breakfast, but he kept trying to eat it with his hands and saying it was good "oatmeal." I fed him as much as he was able to eat—mostly because we had already given him his insulin shots, and even though they'd been running high, I didn't want a sudden drop. He went back to bed but needed help—lots of help. He yelped when Angelo tried to get him into his bed, and he complained of a sharp pain in his hip. He slept most of the day, and we ended up calling the hospice nurse who started him on one of the sedatives that came in the hospice "care package." He had most of a grilled cheese on pumpernickel sandwich and a little yogurt—it ended up being his last meal and not the fettuccine Alfredo with a glass of Würzburger Hofbräu beer I imagined for him.

Once the nurse left, I ran over to a neighbor's to return a dish. She offered me a glass of wine, and who was I to turn that down? I kept an eye on the Dad Cam, and when I saw Angelo wheeling Dad into the bathroom around six, I thought I'd better head back. Dad had asked Angelo to help him get ready for bed. I initially thought I'd try and keep him up— especially since he hadn't eaten anything since his sandwich. But he wasn't interested. He drank some Glucerna and turned in, but he was up the rest of the night, both from restlessness and his dropping blood sugars. I gave him more Glucerna, some orange juice, and a couple of glucose tablets, just to keep it from plummeting.

Sunday. Valentine's Day. Dad woke up agitated, but later that day, he started talking about his life—his "well-lived life." We sat with him on his bed, and he reached out to Angelo to clasp his hand. It was a little like he was meeting him for the first time, and he introduced him to me. Then he spoke more about how grateful he was to have had such love in his life, and he called out, "I still love you, Pattie! Wife of my dreams forever!" He suggested we have a party someday to celebrate all the good he's had in his life. He said he was grateful for the love he's experienced, and I think he thanked me.

The way he spoke to us, and his overall demeanor seemed like he was more comfortable with us than ever. He was funny and smiling. He leaned over to me at one point, and in a stage whisper, asked conspiratorially, "What do we do now?" as if we were at some event where we had to speak or present or something. It was like, here at the end, the old Warren returned to say goodbye. And not just the old Warren—my old dad. The dad I knew growing up, as an awkward child, as a young parent, and as a woman managing a career, family, and obstacles in life. The one who cheered me on and loved me unconditionally. He was back.

Another Monday morning and another startling change was when the case manager/nurse came to check in with Dad and delivered a sobering prognosis: Days, if not hours. I called

Richard immediately and let him know that the flight he was considering for the following Saturday might not get him here in time to say goodbye to Dad. The night before had been a wild one, with the hospice nurse showing up at midnight to administer a medication cocktail. I ended up removing Dad's Dexcom glucose monitor because the stress of wondering what was going to get him first—the low blood sugar coma or the advanced dementia—was grueling. (My curiosity got the best of me on his last day. I tested his blood sugar and it was 164—after no food, no juice, no insulin. Astounding.) All day Monday he slept. He barely moved. I took out his dentures so I could swab his mouth with water mixed with a little Listerine.

That night—or rather the next morning around three, Dad was restless again. I was staying on schedule with his meds, but his sheets were soaked, he was swinging his legs back and forth off the bed, and he needed cleaning. Then he went back to sleep.

Richard had gotten a flight for Tuesday morning, so around midday, I went in to tell Dad that Richard would be here in a couple of hours. I thought just knowing he was on his way might help Dad hang on. I smoothed his hair back from his forehead and whispered, "Richard's on his way. He'll be here in a couple of hours." Dad's eyes popped open!

"What time is it?" And he was up and waiting until Richard walked in the door a few hours later with my brother-in-law and nephew.

The next day—Wednesday, February 17—bumped along typically, at least typically for the previous two weeks. Richard stationed himself in Dad's room, having put a cot in there the night before and sleeping a foot away from him. With Richard on duty, Angelo and I went out for my vaccination, and we took advantage of the free time to stop in for a couple of errands on the way home. At home, I saw that Dad was restless, and his breathing had started sounding gravelly and difficult, although he didn't seem to be in any discomfort from it. I felt I had to find some combination of medications or something to help ease his distress. A few nights earlier, the on-call nurse told me to rub lavender oil and lotion onto the bottoms of his feet, so I tried that again. It seemed to help—for about twenty minutes. After listening to it through dinner, though, I called hospice. It was too frustrating to listen to what sounded like distress. The nurse suggested another dose of morphine. I prepared it and joined Richard at his side to give it to him. But, he spit it out. He was done.

Richard and I sat on either side of the bed, holding his hands and smoothing his hair back. Angelo joined us as Richard and I were telling Dad how much we loved him. When my mom died, the doctor said that hearing is the last function to end, so we kept telling him how much we loved him, and how proud we were to be his children. Angelo told him how grateful we were to have had him with us. And then, with my hand on his heart, Dad was gone.

I don't remember much of how we got through the next few hours, but the hospice nurse showed up, and then the funeral home. A giant of a man gently took control of the situation and assured us he would take good care of Dad. We said goodbye again and again as if he could still hear us.

IN A PERFECT WORLD

"But little Mouse, you are not alone,
In proving foresight may be vain:
The best laid schemes of mice and men
Go often awry,
And leave us nothing but grief and pain,
For promised joy!"

—Robert Burns

After about two years with us, Dad started leaving his shirt untucked when he got dressed for the day. Up until then, he was securely tucked and belted before he'd step foot out of his room. Most of his other typical morning regimen stayed intact, except for when he missed a few hairs from his precision part, and they would straggle into his eyebrows. I first noticed the shirt thing through Mom's eyes: "Why isn't your shirt tucked in today?" I asked when he came out for shots, pills, and breakfast one morning.

"Oh, I don't know. It's easier this way," he'd said, in kind of a tone that didn't invite further discussion. One time, at one of grandson Luca's school events—a holiday concert—I realized that not only had Dad not tucked in his shirt, but there was a huge food-or-soup stain on his black jeans. I saw that through Mom's eyes, too. If he had tried to go to dinner with such a stain when they lived at their apartment, she would have marched him straight back to change. I remember when I'd visit, and Mom would sweep a critical eye over his outfit before leaving for the outside. He became aware of every little drip and spill— nervously so—and seemed to be worried about embarrassing her. I didn't know what the big deal was: Whenever I was in the dining room of their fancy retirement high rise, I noticed *everyone* was spilling and dropping and staining.

As the years went by with Dad living with us, he dropped many of his previous fastidious ways. Not that he became negligent—not him. I continued to be amazed at how often he would preen, taking care to shave every whisker or wipe every morsel from his mouth—often missing both, but the attention was there. He didn't neglect personal hygiene, either, although showers grew fewer and further between, which I chalked up to how difficult it was to manage that particular activity. He needed help, and I was the last person he wanted help from, although I was exactly that person. I started by simply monitoring him from outside his bedroom door and eventually progressed to actually helping him out of the shower and drying off his back since I forbade him from flipping the towel behind him and seesawing it across his back. Too many near-falls forward for that activity anymore.

Dad was on the dementia spectrum, but he was still aware enough to know when he was in the way. His level of care— even if there were times when he insisted that he could take care of himself—prevented us from doing anything spontaneously, long-range, or, for me, income-producing. He had enough savings to prevent him from being a true financial burden, but he didn't have enough to live in an assisted or any other kind of facility, unless he went on Title XIX Medicaid, under which he'd have to divest himself of all his assets and live wherever there was room for him. That option would have come with care that certainly would not have been tailored to his particular personal or medical needs.

Before he died, hospice came in for what we discovered were his last couple of weeks. Hospice threw out all the "maintenance" medications he was on and increased the palliative ones, the drugs that would keep pain and discomfort away from him. We had assistance with bathing him, and we were encouraged to let him eat as much or as little as he desired. Because we had to help him get dressed—and undressed—each day, his wardrobe whittled down to a few pairs of comfy pull-on pants and long-sleeved T-shirts (with a pocket, of course; he had a pocket in his shirt literally to his dying day) to make our job easier. The daily routine of the previous four years went out the window, and a new, more flexible routine was put in place—a routine that was directed by his physical and emotional needs rather than a schedule developed around medications, meals, and about seven doctors' recommendations.

I wish there could be such a place for our elders *before* their last dying weeks or days. Granted, my experience of options available to senior living was limited to Florida and Connecticut (although I did research other areas of the country as well as internationally), but what I found to be the so-called "assisted" living environment wasn't so much assisted as *insisted*. I noticed that the many rules and regulations that protected the staff and facility insisted that the residents change their own needs and habits to comply with the regulations of a corporation. In addition, there isn't much assistance when you walk in the door; there are *tiers* of assistance from which to choose that naturally cost extra the more you add on. As it was, we were encouraged to continue adding to the tiers Dad already had. If he had stayed at the relatively affordable assisted living facility he had already spent three months in, his savings would have drained away. This particular facility was fine; most of the staff appeared genuinely invested in Dad's health and well-being, but their understanding of what that really meant was based on an institutional regimen of care.

What if, at least in our country, we had a hospice-like option for our elders, not just during the last few weeks, but for their remaining years? Where they are cared for as they are and not how a provider or corporation chooses. A place for people like my dad, who needed assistance with some things, but not with others. People whose brains are starting to fail them, but for whom living as independently as possible gives them dignity. What if we didn't expect entire families to turn their lives over to the one person in the world who would choose otherwise? What if our healthcare system could provide a way to honor the senior experience instead of churning out reams of policy and practice? What if funding and research could be devoted to the whole human being, for the breadth of his or her whole life?

Insurance plans that don't cover the aging process for a person is like not including eyes and teeth in health coverage plans: ridiculous. There are families that are lucky to have more resources and money, which afford them more choices in how to care for their aging loved ones. But there are millions of people whose families simply need more options. It is taking a long time for healthcare to catch up to the needs of Americans, and I am not convinced that a program for taking care of our elder population is on the horizon. No, I have no delusions that this will happen in my lifetime. The experience with my dad has brought me to understand how important it is to take care of myself and plan for my old age.

But of course, my dad did that, too.

AT THE COTTAGE ALONE

"Alone again. Naturally."
—GILBERT O'SULLIVAN

"**B**ut you already went to Maine!" exclaimed a friend after
I posted my second arrival at the island in just under ten
days to Facebook. Angelo and I had come up together to
open the cottage and stayed a few days afterward, but when
it was time to return home, I couldn't get past the feeling of
wanting just to stay. We even talked about whether or not
it was doable—and I decided it wasn't. So, we returned for
a couple of events at home. But then I came back. Solo. The
pull of having time alone was too strong. I had been talking
about the need to be alone for years—as long as I had been
caring for Dad in our home. This was my opportunity to get
that kind of time. Angelo would cover picking up Luca from
school, and also be on-call for any other Papa-duty, so there
was really no reason I shouldn't go—except I kept feeling like
I was sneaking out of my house. Like when I was a teenager
and I didn't want anyone to find out where I was going or
what I was doing.

A few years ago, I ran into an old friend who had just recently lost her father. She told me that her care coordinator advised her to take some time after the loss—at least six weeks. So, she went on an extended trip to London, Paris, and Rome for a couple of months, staying with friends or bed and breakfasts as she traveled. At the time, I thought to myself with no small amount of sour grapes, "Yeah, that's probably what I'll do, too." I was only a couple years in having Dad live with us, but I already knew it was wearing me down. (Apologies to all my friends who thought I changed my name to Exhausted because all I said for the last five years was, "I'm exhausted.") I knew I needed time alone but didn't know how to make it happen. Now here was that opportunity.

My plan was what it always is: Get some writing done. And reading. I imagined myself spending day after day reading all of the six books I brought with me and getting lots of words into my current manuscript. I was going to take walks, eat healthy, and get some rest. I didn't even know when I was going to come back; all I knew was that I was going. I had a plan. And we all know what happens to plans.

One of the first things that I realized was that being there—alone—gave space to all the emotions that I'd been holding at bay for one reason or another. My mom was the first to show up. I am known to drink my coffee every morning out of a mug I brought up years earlier and left there for that purpose. The memory of the mug's arrival came to me: Once, after I arrived to visit them, Mom pointed to "my" mug sitting squarely on the kitchen counter and said, "What's this?" Apparently, its presence hadn't been approved by the management (Mom) and was in danger of losing a spot in the cabinet.

Then came Susie. Memories of her poked their way into my stay. We had come up together one year to get it ready for renters. We used to pretend we were at a writers' retreat

to justify our sitting on the deck all day long, smoking ciga-
rettes, and drinking coffee—and writing. It was also the site
of our biggest blowup: a months-long disagreement that I
think shocked both of us even after we made up and forgave
each other.

And of course, Dad was there. We have this place because
of him. His handwriting is everywhere, from the list of steps on
how to open and close the cottage to the labels on the pegboard
in the shed that indicate where each tool goes.

I'm sure I've explained that our "cottage" is nothing more
than a winterized fishing camp, and even "winterized" is too
strong a word. It's the view that keeps us coming back—and
the repairs. If it's not one thing it's another with this place.
The latest project was to move the shed out of the middle of
the driveway where it landed two years ago as if a twister had
picked it up and moved it intact when the septic system was
replaced. I didn't have to move the shed—the excavator did
that—but I did have to empty it and then put all the stuff
back afterward.

I did things I never thought I would have to do.

In an essay from my first book, I wrote about old dogs
and new tricks and how I probably wouldn't be acquiring any
new skills with any proficiency—and how I was fine with that.
But I did new tricks! One thing I did was put together a list
of chores for the other family members to do when they came
up to the cottage. The list ranged from slapping a coat of paint
on the front of the house to hoisting the foundation up to sit
back on the sauna tubes it was originally settled on. I also had
a box full of notes, files, and bills, and I decided to sort out
what we still needed from what I could safely toss. Like an old
phone bill when we didn't even have a phone anymore. As I
rummaged among the piles of documents we'd saved over the
years, I came across this photo.

There we were. My family—as we began. From left to right Susie, my Dad, and my Mom are gone. Richard, in the middle, and I are left. Two-fifths of our family. That's when I finally lost it.

There is no shortage of writing about grief. For every nuance of the process, there is a book, movie, song, article, or expert on it from which to find affirmation and empathy.

I've been buffeted by emotions, sadness, loss, anger, and just flat-out craziness. It's been hard, but I'm so grateful I have been able to be present for it. Because isn't this what it's all about? We feel, we lose, we cry, we resent. I expect my body and my heart to go through this, and I don't want to miss a minute.

After only a few days, I felt as though I'd been alone at the cottage for at least a month or more. When I thought about going home, I felt ready. I believe there are still many steps on this path.

I'm ready to take them.

IN THE END

"*Do not pity the dead, Harry. Pity the living.*
And above all, those who live without love."
—ALBUS DUMBLEDORE

A t the very last moment, just as they're about to go, there
is really only that one thing left—love. At that precise
moment, for me at least, the previous caregiving years full of
stress and emotions and hardship simply fell away, and the great
love I always felt for my dad was available to me so that I could
express all that he meant to me as he passed on.

And even though I didn't actually know that would
happen, I somehow knew that it might. It's the reason why
I was compelled to record—and share—the caregiving
experience I had while I was living it. I mean—I'd be writing
about it anyway, but the idea to create a kind of record about
it while it was happening came to me early—and not just
because I wanted to publish another book. In fact, these essays
only became a book later on; my initial idea was to share the
experiences I was having as an ongoing discussion board or
through a social media outlet.

I expect that there are some who will read the essays in this book and decide I'm an ungrateful child if not a full-on terrible person. (Those people probably already stopped reading anyway.) As difficult as it was to expose my darker thoughts and less-than-stellar behaviors, I can also say I learned much about myself and others throughout the years of caring for my dad. The responsibility for caring for another human being is interconnected with other responsibilities in ways that often go unnoticed. It's not like caring for a child at all and I think that comparison is irresponsible. It creates some kind of notion that it is somehow a natural occurrence in our lives. But it's not. Of course, everyone will have their own unique experience due to the individual personalities of each person and the family history and dynamics involved, but when someone says, "Well, they took care of us, blah, blah blah," it negates the distinct and important task that one is being called—or expected—to do.

There are a lot of other feelings and emotions that compound a caregiver's experience: guilt, obligation, fear, responsibility, gratitude, grief. During the years we cared for Dad, I read and heard a lot about guilt. I've written about it myself. Guilt infuses itself throughout obvious and subtle aspects of most relationships, but there's none so insidious as the guilt one feels when he or she feels terrible taking care of our needy parents. It's already a hard job. Do we have to feel guilty, too? It's not enough that guilt is generated by our own feelings of resentment and self-pity; depending on your upbringing or religious community, some guilt is inbred. But our society imposes it upon us, too. If you've never been admonished by a receptionist or doctor—or any stranger for that matter who doesn't have a clue about your life or your relationship with your loved one—then you're lucky. I've been the target of suspicious stares and outright accusations that I wasn't doing right by my dad. There were times when I was afraid someone would report me for elder abuse—and I *knew* I was doing a good job. It's one of the coldest and most unfeeling accusations ever—that of a disbelieving professional judging your ability to care for your dad. It gives rise to the immediate "I know I'm doing a bad job—does *everyone* have to point it out?" feeling of guilt.

And fear. What if I *am* doing a terrible job? Am I the worst person in the world to take on this responsibility? Who else would do it if I don't? There wasn't anyone. So, I did it and I imposed the obligation on the rest of my family while I neglected their needs, too. There were days I was a mess feeling guilty for the complete disaster I created when I chose to bring my dad home to live with us.

But at some point during the experience, my lived experience, I became aware of the fact that I didn't have to feel guilty. Not only that, but it became important to me to not feel guilty about anything I was doing. Why in the world should guilt play a part in what I—and my entire family—was experiencing? None of us—especially me and my dad—should feel guilty about anything. And so I didn't. And I still don't.

And that is exactly why I wrote down all that I was feeling during the time he was with us. I recorded all the impatience, anger, frustration, annoyance, and guilt specifically for this purpose—to present a whole picture of what it is like to care for a parent in your home. My picture won't be like everyone's picture—varying levels of dementia, ability, financial options, and family support will create each individual situation. But what I do know is that it is hard, and it takes a toll on a family, whether or not everyone's laughing and joking all the time or mired in old dynamics and resentment.

I also knew that I might tend to "clean up" any really nasty feelings or descriptions of the things I had to do in service to caregiving after my dad was gone because I would be guided by grief and wanting to present a more cheerful picture than the one I had just been through.

I believe that I was able to be fully present for my dad when he died because I allowed myself to rid myself of guilt. Love was able to take over when it was most important when I could make sure he passed on knowing he was loved. When he died, although it was just the four of us together—Angelo, Richard, Dad, and me—I told him that everyone's love was in the room. Mom, Susie, Annie, Christopher, Tony, Luca, Justine, Maddie, Aiden, John, Stephan, Diane, Charlie, and Brigitte. All our love was in the room, including his. No regrets, no anger, no guilt. Because, in the end, my dad would be the last person who would want me to feel guilty. Because he loved me.

SIX MONTHS LATER

"Whether it's the best of times or the worst of times,
it's the only time we've got."
—Art Buchwald

On the six-month anniversary of my dad's death, the first thing that hit me was just that: it had been six months since he died. Six months. It seemed both so long ago and just yesterday. The day—the seventeenth—repeats itself over and over in our family's special days. My children's birthdays are on the seventeenth, and my daughter was born seventeen months after I married her dad on August 17. That date, the seventeenth, triggered the realization of how my grief had changed; I found I was actually missing him where before I was simply getting over his death.

Realizing how long it had been since he died also made me recognize that turning point in how I felt about his death. The first six months were characterized by a numbness and a feeling of not being sure *how* I felt after such a long time of caring for him. I still didn't feel comfortable leaving the house—pandemic or not. When I did go out, I felt like I couldn't stay out—I had to get home to him. And when at home, I continued to jump if I heard something fall in the house or an unidentified noise at night. My days were governed by an unknown and arbitrary schedule, somewhat like when he was alive, but now mostly imaginary as my awareness wasn't actually needed for any particular reason. I just remained vigilant.

The turning point began as a feeling of sadness when I thought of him, rather than tension or stress or the feeling that I hadn't finished taking care of his affairs. Which I hadn't. Feeling sadness about my dad wasn't new; it punctuated the entire time he was with us. Angelo and I often remarked about how sorry we felt for him—such a remarkable man trapped in such a frustrating situation. It was sad to see him be so angry at himself for dropping his spoon or forgetting an old friend's name. But it was also stressful. The angry self-talk he indulged in so often was hard to be around, but it also gave me some insight into my own self-negativity. Sadness wasn't a strange feeling, just one that was often mixed with others—like exhaustion, stress, and impatience.

But sadness was the entrée into the part of me that was beginning to miss him. After the six-month mark, I began remembering the before-times. Like the time he woke up from his coma and the doctor quietly asked him, "Warren, can you move your arm?" And he suddenly flung his arm up in the air, pumping it up and down several times to make sure we saw it.

Or the time he took my collect phone call after I went to visit my first husband's family in San Francisco at Christmas and the trip turned into a family drama of epic proportions. I called my dad, and he said, "Just come home." He bought me a plane ticket, and I did. I remember him always with Annie, Christopher, and my nephew John and how totally focused he was when he was with them—playing a game, taking them shopping, and having them "help" doing yardwork.

And always in Maine: reading on the deck, working the *New York Times* crossword with Mom, always fixing, or painting or improving something, and just loving being there, mostly when we were all there with him.

There are a lot of "I wish . . ." moments that come up for me now. I wish it didn't have to be like that, I wish we had more time, I wish I hadn't been so impatient, so intolerant of his repetitive complaints and previously unknown arrogance. When my thoughts wander in that direction and I start to regret all of the arguments, misunderstandings, and impatience, I recall how difficult it actually was. For almost four years—and even the months after Dad died—I rarely got a full night's sleep. He fought his disability almost unconsciously and couldn't be aware of all the ways that he needed care and supervision. Angelo's and my life together—and all the ways in which I was a part of my children's lives—were curtailed or made nonexistent. We couldn't even go out to run errands together, much less take a trip or run out for a drink. And our income rested entirely on Angelo's shoulders, as there was no way I could work even part-time. I had a full-time job.

I suppose the biggest wish I have is that we had more options in our country to care for our elders. I hated that the opportunity to care for my dad was made much, much harder because of a lack of resources. That's why, even when I wish it had been different, I don't feel guilty that it wasn't. Taking on the care of another human being is an enormous amount of pressure to put on one person—because it is often one person for whom the bulk of the responsibility falls—and other than in rare cases, it can't be any other way. The loved one isn't happy to be a burden and the caregiver isn't happy to have his or her life appropriated. Still, I also know we were lucky to do what we did; we did the best we could do—Angelo, me, and Dad. Every day. And, ironically, we wouldn't have had it any other way.

Years ago, when we all lived close by in the same small town in Connecticut, we decided to go out to eat at a local restaurant for dinner. Dad was still at work, so I picked up my mom and sister at their house and with three-year-old Annie in tow, we headed to grab a table at a popular tavern. Dad would meet us there. It was busy that night, and, as we settled in (all talking and looking at the menu and providing crayons and paper for Annie), I looked up for some reason and caught sight of a man walking in the entrance near the hostess stand. His appearance struck me, and I thought, "Well, *he's* handsome," and a split second later, I realized it was Dad! He didn't command the room when he walked in but possessed a subtle confidence as he made his way over to us. It was weird and startling to observe briefly, as a stranger, how others might see Dad, and the experience has stayed with me ever since. He joined us seamlessly as he kissed Mom hello and sat down, then began *oohing* and *ahhing* at Annie's drawings and checked the menu to find a special appetizer for us. His presence that night—and almost every time I can remember—brought a sense of accord; it was like the grown-up had arrived and we could all relax. We would be taken care of.

That's what he did—took care of us. And that's why his living with us was so difficult for him. Even though he instilled in me the same deeply responsible obligation to care for and protect the ones we love, it was nearly impossible for him to hand that over to me so I could care for him. Instead, our time together was challenging in so many ways, ways that could only be the way they were. There was no "if only things were different" for us. What we had, what we were experiencing, was the way it was, the only way it could be, given who each of us were.

The time that has passed has allowed me to be more present for my feelings and love for him. And now, I really miss my dad. I miss his sense of humor and his intelligence. I miss knowing there was one person in the whole world I could count on to be in my corner unquestionably. I miss his exactness and his lists and his sense of order. I miss his laugh, and even his sarcasm.

I just miss him.

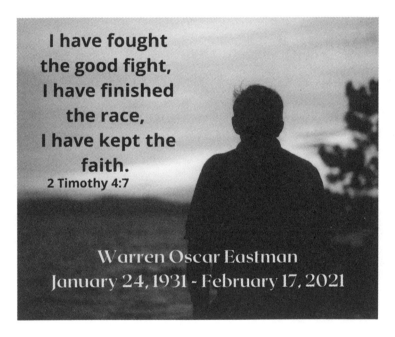

I have fought the good fight, I have finished the race, I have kept the faith.
2 Timothy 4:7

Warren Oscar Eastman
January 24, 1931 - February 17, 2021

ACKNOWLEDGMENTS

Writing a book is a solitary task; publishing one is not. I'd like to thank the following, my book village, for helping me bring this book into existence.

To begin, as always, Warren, Pattie, Richard, and Susie. And then, Annie, Christopher, Justine, Angelo and John and Stephan. Who in turn have brought Tony, Luca, Maddie, Aiden, Kolette, Kelli, and Aria into my life. The richness of love and support from my family is constant and true. Even as I focused on my own experience of caregiving throughout these essays, I know how deeply the experience impacted all of my family. I remember texting with Annie a few weeks after Dad died about being able to spend the day with her and Luca. I said I was really happy to be able to do it, and she replied, "Me too; I really missed it." There were so many ways in which all our lives changed—not all good, but not all bad either. I like to believe that we all grew closer and gained a deeper understanding of what being a member of a family really means.

My friend Trudy was, as always, my sherpa throughout both the caregiving years and getting this book done.

Brooke Warner, Crystal Patriarche, Lauren Wise, Tabitha Bailey and She Writes Press sisters—I can't say enough about the She Writes Press community, but I'll try. She Writes Press and Booksparks are not just companies. They are beacons of opportunity for women's voices and experiences. The integrity, intelligence, and fierceness with which every story is respected, guided, and brought into existence is nonpareil in—I would imagine—any business setting. But it's especially gratifying when sharing a life story such as mine.

I facilitate a couple of writing groups and there came a time when I wondered who was facilitating who! All the writers I've "taught" or worked with played a role in supporting me with their feedback or even their presence. But most especially, the Hamsters.

Roberto was the surprise copyeditor I didn't know I needed. What a gift his talents and beautiful feelings were in helping shape this book into what it became.

And finally my deepest gratitude to my dad, Warren. Neither of us could imagine in our wildest dreams that life would turn out like this. I will never know how you felt about it, but I remain grateful to be your daughter and your caregiver.

ABOUT THE AUTHOR

Cindy Eastman is an award-winning author whose first book, *Flip-Flops After 50: And Other Thoughts On Aging I Remembered To Write Down*, is a collection of humorous essays about aging. She is also a contributor to several anthologies including the *Fast Women* series edited by Gina Barreca and published by Woodhall Press. She writes a weekly column on getting older called *Silver Linings* on Substack and monthly column with her daughter, Annie Musso, for Hearst Media.

She is the creator of the Writual writing program and has presented nationally at the Story Circle Network Women's Writing Conference as well as having been a featured speaker on a number of panels and programs. Cindy has a master's degree in education and is currently an adjunct at Naugatuck Valley Community College teaching English. You can contact Cindy or read more of her work at cindyeastman.com.

Author photo © Annie Musso

Looking for your next great read?

We can help!

Visit www.shewritespress.com/next-read
or scan the QR code below for a list
of our recommended titles.

She Writes Press is an award-winning
independent publishing company founded to
serve women writers everywhere.